DEVELOPING A LEARNING CULTURE

Latest titles in the McGraw-Hill Training Series

EVALUATING TRAINING EFFECTIVENESS 2nd edition
Benchmarking your Training Activity Against Best Practice
Peter Bramley   ISBN 0-07-709028-4
DEVELOPING A LEARNING CULTURE
Empowering People to Deliver Quality, Innovation and Long-term Success
Sue Jones   ISBN 0-07-707983-3
THE CREATIVE TRAINER
Holistic Facilitation Skills for Accelerated Learning
Michael Lawlor and Peter Handley   ISBN 0-07-709030-6
DEVELOPING EFFECTIVE TRAINING SKILLS 2nd edition
A Practical Guide to Designing and Delivering Group Training
Tony Pont   ISBN 0-07-709143-4
CROSS-CULTURAL TEAM BUILDING
Guidelines for More Effective Communication and Negotiation
Mel Berger   ISBN 0-07-7077919-1
LEARNING TO CHANGE
A Resource for Trainers, Managers and Learners Based on Self-Organised Learning
Sheila Harri-Augstein and Ian M. Webb   ISBN 0-07-707896-9
ASSESSMENT AND DEVELOPMENT IN EUROPE
Adding Value to Individuals and Organizations
Edited by Mac Bolton   ISBN 0-07-707928-0
PRACTICAL INSTRUCTIONAL DESIGN FOR OPEN LEARNING
MATERIALS
A Modular Course Covering Open Learning, Computer-based Training and Multi-
media
Nigel Harrison   ISBN 0-07-709055-1
DELIVERING IN-HOUSE OUTPLACEMENT
A Practical Guide for Trainers, Managers and Personnel Specialists
Alan Jones   ISBN 0-07-707895-0
FACILITATION
Providing Opportunities For Learning
Trevor Bentley   ISBN 0-07-707684-2
DEVELOPMENT CENTRES
Realizing the Potential of Your Employees Through Assessment and Development
Geoff Lee and David Beard   ISBN 0-07-707785-7
DEVELOPING DIRECTORS
Building an Effective Boardroom Team
Colin Coulson-Thomas   ISBN 0-07-707590-0
MANAGING THE TRAINING PROCESS
Putting the Basics into Practice
Mike Wills   ISBN 0-07-707806-3
RESOURCE-BASED LEARNING
Using Open and Flexible Resources for Continuous Development
Julie Dorrell   ISBN 0-07-707692-3

Details of these and other titles in the series are available from:

The Product Manager, Professional Books, McGraw-Hill Book Company Europe,
Shoppenhangers Road, Maidenhead, Berkshire SL6 2QL, United Kingdom
Tel: 01628 23432 Fax: 01628 770224

Developing a learning culture

Empowering people to deliver quality, innovation and long-term success

Sue Jones

McGRAW-HILL BOOK COMPANY

London · New York · St Louis · San Francisco · Auckland
Bogotá · Caracas · Lisbon · Madrid · Mexico · Milan
Montreal · New Delhi · Panama · Paris · San Juan · São Paulo
Singapore · Sydney · Tokyo · Toronto

Published by
McGRAW-HILL Book Company Europe
Shoppenhangers Road, Maidenhead, Berkshire, SL6 2QL, England
Telephone: 01628 23432
Fax: 01628 770224

British Library Cataloguing in Publication Data
Jones, Susan
    Developing a Learning Culture: Empowering
People to Deliver Quality, Innovation
and Long-term Success. — (McGraw-Hill
Training Series)
I. Title   II. Series
658.3124

    ISBN 0-07-707983-3

Library of Congress Cataloging-in-Publication Data
Jones, Sue.
    Developing a learning culture: empowering people to deliver
quality, innovation, and long-term success / Sue Jones.
        p.   cm. — (McGraw-Hill training series)
    Includes index.
    ISBN 0-07-707983-3 (paperback)
    1. Organizational learning. 2. Employee empowerment. 3. Success
in business.   I. Title.   II. Series.
HD58.82.J66   1996
658.3'124—dc20
                                                                            95-43686
                                                                            CIP

McGraw-Hill

A Division of The McGraw-Hill Companies

Reprinted 1997

Typeset by BookEns Limited, Baldock, Herts.
and printed and bound in Great Britain at the University Press, Cambridge

Printed on permanent paper in compliance with ISO Standard 9706

Contents

Series preface

Training and development are now firmly centre stage in most organizations, if not all. Nothing unusual in that—for some organizations. They have always seen training and development as part of the heart of their businesses—but more and more must see it that same way.

The demographic trends through the 1990s will inject into the marketplace severe competition for good people who will need good training. Young people without conventional qualifications, skilled workers in redundant crafts, people out of work, women wishing to return to work—all will require excellent training to fit them to meet the job demands of the 1990s and beyond.

But excellent training does not spring from what we have done well in the past. T&D specialists are in a new ball game. 'Maintenance' training—training to keep up skill levels to do what we have always done—will be less in demand. Rather, organization, work and market change training are now much more important and will remain so for some time. Changing organizations and people is no easy task, requiring special skills and expertise which, sadly, many T&D specialists do not possess.

To work as a 'change' specialist requires us to get to centre stage—to the heart of the company's business. This means we have to ask about future goals and strategies, and even be involved in their development, at least as far as T&D policies are concerned.

This demands excellent communication skills, political expertise, negotiating ability, diagnostic skills—indeed, all the skills a good internal consultant requires.

The implications for T&D specialists are considerable. It is not enough merely to be skilled in the basics of training, we must also begin to act like business people and to think in business terms and talk the language of business. We must be able to resource training not just from within but by using the vast array of external resources. We must be able to manage our activities as well as any other manager. We must share in the creation and communication of the company's vision. We must never let the goals of the company out of our sight.

In short, we may have to grow and change with the business. It will be hard. We shall have to demonstrate not only relevance but also value for money and achievement of results. We shall be our own boss, as accountable for results as any other line manager, and we shall have to deal with fewer internal resources.

The challenge is on, as many T&D specialists have demonstrated to me over the past few years. We need to be capable of meeting that challenge. This is why McGraw-Hill Book Company Europe have planned and launched this major new training series—to help us meet that challenge.

The series covers all aspects of T&D and provides the knowledge base from which we can develop plans to meet the challenge. They are practical books for the professional person. They are a starting point for planning our journey into the twenty-first century.

Use them well. Don't just read them. Highlight key ideas, thoughts, action pointers or whatever, and have a go at doing something with them. Through experimentation we evolve; through stagnation we die.

I know that all the authors in the McGraw-Hill Training Series would want me to wish you good luck. Have a great journey into the twenty-first century.

ROGER BENNETT
Series Editor

About the series editor

Roger Bennett has over 20 years' experience in training, management education, research and consulting. He has long been involved with trainer training and trainer effectiveness. He has carried out research into trainer effectiveness, and conducted workshops, seminars, and conferences on the subject around the world. He has written extensively on the subject including the book *Improving Trainer Effectiveness*, Gower. His work has taken him all over the world and has involved directors of companies as well as managers and trainers.

Dr Bennett has worked in engineering, several business schools (including the International Management Centre, where he launched the UK's first masters degree in T&D), and has been a board director of two companies. He is the editor of the *Journal of European Industrial Training* and was series editor of the ITD's *Get In There* workbook and video package for the managers of training departments. He now runs his own business called The Management Development Consultancy.

About the author

Sue Jones has over 25 years' experience in education and training. Her background is multi-disciplinary, working as a research scientist at university and ICI, before undertaking a Masters degree in philosophy. She has lectured in Further Education, written a number of teaching programmes for use in Higher Education, and piloted participatory training approaches for practising teachers. Her research and writings cover topics such as perception, inductive learning, computer-assisted learning, and collaborative training and management practices. Dr Jones now works as a freelance lecturer and writer, and is an associate director of Education Now Ltd.

Acknowledgements

I would like to thank all those organizations and people named in the book who have given interviews, provided material, and responded to drafts of short abstracts with useful information.

I would also like to acknowledge my debt to Professor Matthew Lipman's work on 'communities of enquiry' in education and training; and to thank Professor Roland and Janet Meighan, and Philip and Annabel Toogood for the opportunity to be involved in their pioneering work promoting democratic education and training.

Introduction

Anglo-Saxon countries have had a relatively poor education and training record compared to competitor countries in Europe and the Far East. There tends to be lower educational performance, less training, and much of the training that does occur is often not effective, leading to tremendous financial waste. It is essential for the survival of companies that the cause of this disadvantageous comparison is addressed, and people's potential to create the improved efficiency and added-value necessary to meet rapidly increasing global competition is mobilized.

This book looks at the cultural dimensions of learning and training. It considers how the 'anti-learning anti-training' situation still prevalent in English-speaking countries, stems from aspects of the traditional hierarchical organizational, financial and governmental cultures; aspects which previously have been neglected or considered to be of little significance to either learning or training.

Terms such as 'employee involvement', 'empowerment', 'teamwork', 'total quality management' (TQM), 'customer care', etc., became so familiar in the 1980s that already by the early 1990s some people began to see them as 'old hat' and offering 'nothing new' to the workplace. Yet, in most British, American, and other English-speaking countries, there has been a big gap between this management rhetoric and the reality of the shop-floor. The goals represented by the rhetoric have, in fact, systematically been undermined by a prevailing hierarchical financially-driven culture, characterized by the following interrelated features:

- Focusing on maximizing short-term profit, share price and dividend, cost-cutting, private gain, mergers and acquisitions, at the expense of developing the underlying operating business through investment in training, equipment, and R&D.
- Championing of a de-humanized, cost-oriented, adversarial management approach with employees, suppliers and customers, creating an environment of exclusion, attrition and insecurity.
- Obstruction of a more equal-footing—what variously is called 'democratic', 'reciprocal', 'collaborative' or 'inclusive'—relationship with all stakeholders needed for shared decision-making, long-term

commitment and trust, adopted by more innovative and successful competitors.

- Marginalization, and block on the development, of core interpersonal attitudes and skills which underpin effective reciprocal relationships.

The persistence of this traditional 'command and control' culture has been helped by Western TQ philosophy which has failed adequately to address key interpersonal skills needed to deliver the rhetoric. The book identifies core interpersonal attitudes and related 'skills' at the root of the traditional hierarchical culture, and considers how they create unequal 'power-based' relationships which undermine learning, training, and performance. They are considered to be endemic not only in organizational and financial managers, but also external trainers, academics and consultants, and give rise to:

- Little to no value put on the reciprocal involvement and development of *every* employee/trainee as the basis for high performance and innovation.
- A failure to understand the crucial influence of an organization's culture (the nature of relationships and underlying attitudes and values) and structure on the potential for continuous learning and cost-effective training.
- A failure to recognize the overriding influence of the top manager (CEO) on an organization's culture and structure.
- A failure to understand the fundamental importance of these links to customer satisfaction and long-term competitiveness.

The outcome has been managers who oversee no or wasteful training, and who ineffectively deploy quality programmes and HR techniques as *add-ons* to the traditional culture, leaving the hierarchical 'power-based' management employee relationship intact; and trainers and consultants who facilitate this. A major claim of the book, therefore, is that unless the culture issue is addressed effectively, then in general:

- Training will not be cost-effective.
- Managers will continue to deploy quality programmes and systems (e.g. TQM, BS 5750) and HRM techniques (e.g. employee involvement, single status, organizational flexibility), ineffectively and counterproductively to increase control.
- Related educational and training programmes in quality, teamwork and leadership, will continue to be little more than highly expensive tinkerings on the margins.

The generally poor education and training record, high failure rate of Total Quality initiatives and Human Resource techniques, and resultant low position in developed countries' competitiveness league tables—certainly in Britain and to a certain extent in America—is testimony to the importance of the above links and the widespread failure to recognize them.

There is growing awareness in certain top managers and writers of the importance of some of the above factors. They rightly condemn endemic mission statements and management rhetoric which exist alongside conflicting management actions. However, the criticism tends to be fragmentary and generalized, and to lack:

- A full consideration of core interpersonal attitudes and skills and their fundamental relevance to the link between the top manager, organizational culture, learning and performance.
- An awareness of the need for a structured approach to core skills development.
- A clear indication of what top managers must do to create a learning and innovation-enhancing culture.
- How they can do it.

As a consequence those top managers who have begun to make effective culture changes, generally still have one step further to go to develop a fully collaborative learning organization. The aim of this book is:

- To give a fuller and clearer exposition of the above links and requirements.
- To consider cultural and structural priorities for training and HR managers, and the key role of these personnel in culture change.
- To provide an integrated training–working vehicle which simultaneously builds the reciprocal relationships vital for continuous learning, cost-effective training, and the improved performance and competitiveness they enable.

In this way the book hopes to provide practical support for a wide range of people involved in training and personnel functions. This would span training, HR and senior managers and consultants responsible for strategic training and development design, planning and implementation; in-house trainers, line managers, team leaders, external trainers and lecturers, responsible for particular training needs identification and delivery; and enlightened business managers and entrepreneurs who want to increase the use of employee initiatives and self-reliance.

1 The competitive case for knowledge and skills

This chapter will consider the case for education and training by indicating:

- Why the view that competitiveness mainly depends on low costs, particularly low labour costs, is mistaken
- Why both employers and government need to focus on developing knowledge and skills as a key factor in an organization's and country's competitiveness.

Low skills and uncompetitiveness

The limitations of cost-competitiveness

A prevailing belief among business leaders in Britain, America and increasingly Western European countries is:

Belief A

The way to be competitive and win orders at home and abroad is to cut labour costs.

This view has been heightened by the competitive threat posed in the global market place by emerging low-wage economies in Asia, Eastern Europe and South America, which has been an increasing cause for concern in Western companies. Low labour costs, it is believed, will stem the tide of company contractions and collapses against competition from low-wage countries.

The relatively high non-wage 'add-on' social costs of labour which employers have to meet in many continental European countries compared to countries such as America, Britain and Japan, are a justifiable cause for concern for the former countries. However, the general meaning of belief A by those who expound it, particularly in Britain and America, is that labour costs need to be reduced through cutting add-on social costs *and* through lower pay. But one only has to consider the exporting success of high-wage economies such as (West) Germany and Japan (Figure 1.1), to realize the mistakenness of belief A. As one commentator aptly put it when arguing against the view that people in the West are being put out of work by being 'underbid' by people in low-wage countries: 'if that was the case everyone in Germany would have been put out of work by the rest of the world some time ago'.

	Manufacturing labour costs (US$ per hour)	*UK trade deficit* (£ billion)
Germany (West)	25.56	3.708
Japan	19.20	5.883
UK	12.82	

Figure 1.1 *Comparative labour costs and UK trade deficits*
Source: US Department of Labor/DTI, 1993

Why belief A is mistaken

Put very simply, three of the main reasons why belief A is mistaken are as follows:

1 As far as costs go, it is not labour costs as such that are relevant to the customer, but the cost of the product, or cost per unit output. Therefore, the more efficient your processes, i.e. the more you can produce for any particular level of:
(a) labour
(b) materials
(c) energy
(d) machine-time
(e) fixed costs (factory, building, plant, etc.)
the lower the cost per unit output, and also the lower the unit labour cost (cost of labour per unit of output). So it is these two efficiency factors which are the relevant 'cost' measures for the customer. Also, of these two measures, it is the cost per unit output rather than the unit labour cost which is the more important factor. For example, if wages drop, people are likely to have reduced morale and be less efficient and are more wasteful in machine-time, materials, energy, etc. It is possible that the 'gain' in lowering labour costs is balanced by a loss in productivity (output per worker), leaving the unit labour cost the same, but the overall costs (due to increased inefficiency, increased waste, etc.), and therefore the cost per unit output, will be increased. Furthermore, attempts to lower unit labour costs through job cuts or measures such as increased automation combined with job cuts, will not necessarily in the long-run have the beneficial effect

on productivity, i.e. output per employee, and so on unit labour cost, as might be expected.

Note According to accountants Ernst and Young, labour costs in Britain are among the lowest in Europe but productivity is also one of the lowest.

Labour costs are relevant but not the main cost factor.
Low wages are often associated with low efficiency and productivity.
Efficiency (cost per unit output) is the most important cost measure.

(See also Example 1, Chapter 7.)

2 Western economies are unlikely ever to match the 'cost per unit output' levels of very low-wage countries, however efficient and productive they become, because of great differences not just in pay levels (which can be in the order of 10 to 100 times less), but also in the price of other things that go to making up the total cost of the product, e.g. labour costs in many major manufacturers account for only about one-tenth of their total cost of production.

It is unrealistic to expect to compete with very low-wage countries on the basis of cost measures alone.

---

3 It is not just cost but also 'added-value' which is important for the customer. Given a choice, generally customers will pay more for products which are better quality, more reliable, more sophisticated and innovative, and better designed to satisfy their needs and requirements.[1] Of course, if the costs of goods are on a par, people will choose the product with the greatest added-value, i.e. superior quality and innovation. More efficient and innovative companies will be able to combine competitive prices with higher added-value.

Cost measures are important but not the only competitive factor.
Added-value is a key competitive factor.

On the basis of the above three reasons, therefore, the general message for Western countries and organizations is:

Belief B

The way to be competitive and win orders at home and abroad is to maximize efficiency and add value.

Low pay, low skills, low competitiveness

There are two ways in which low pay leads to low efficiency and low added-value, and therefore low competitiveness:

1 Low pay leads to low morale, high staff turnover and a low commitment to the organization and to improving efficiency and quality, etc.
   (*Note* Chapter 4 considers a major factor besides pay which influences morale and motivation, and its consequent effect on competitiveness.)
2 Low pay is linked with low skills, and poor paying employers tend to offer poor conditions and no training.

The next section considers why low skills will not deliver the efficiency and added-value necessary for competitiveness.

High skills and added-value

Added-value and efficiency

Value can be added to a product, whether a manufactured product or a service 'product', through the following main routes:

- quality
- innovation
- service
  - speed (meeting orders, market trends, etc.);
  - close customer–supplier relationship (within companies, between companies and with end customer), to give quick responsiveness to customers' needs;
  - knowledge of the product.

These routes overlap. Furthermore, the routes to added-value overlap with the routes to improved efficiency and productivity. Points of overlap include the following:

- An increase in product quality (whether manufactured or service 'product') which leads to more efficient work processes through fewer mistakes, less rework, less waste, fewer delays, better use of machine-time and materials, leading to reduced costs and improved efficiency, productivity and speed (Deming, 1986, p.3).
- A close customer–supplier relationship enables a:
  - commitment to investment by the supplier;
  - pooling of knowledge and skills;
  - focusing on exact requirements through integrated design, lowering

costs, cutting out uncertainty, improving quality, catalysing innovation, and again reducing waste, rework, etc., reducing inventories and removing unnecessary links in the chain, improving efficiency, productivity and speed.

- A close customer–supplier relationship enables feedback and speedy identification and resolution of problems, which improves efficiency and product and service quality (see e.g. Milliken and Rank Xerox examples, Chapter 4), and which can lead to innovations in working practices.

Note Close collaboration between customer and supplier, where the benefits are equally shared—often absent in the UK and US—is a key feature of Japanese competitiveness. Toyota, for example, gives greatest priority to those suppliers who are closest in terms of information sharing, cooperation and staff exchanges. Nissan requires its suppliers to work closely with them, and has a Supplier Development Team for that purpose.

The skills route to added-value and efficiency

The only way to maximize efficiency and the above routes to added-value is to have a skilled and knowledgeable workforce. Relating to the growth in technology, for example, there will need to be:

- Appropriate technical knowledge and skills to be able to use the increasingly high tech equipment needed for the efficiency gains and added-value this equipment enables, both in the manufacturing and service sectors.
- Appropriate technical knowledge and skills to be able to manufacture high tech products (see below).

Most importantly there will need to be:

- Broader 'core' skills which provide the major foundation for acquiring, applying and continuously updating technical knowledge and skills, and the ideas and judgement necessary for effectively delivering efficiency and the above routes to added-value (see below and Chapter 4).

Ideas for improvement

Machines do not have ideas. Whatever advances new technology enables, and whatever other assets a company has, it is people upon which that advance depends. Only people can come up with the ideas for the new technology in the first place, and it is people on which the effective and imaginative use of that technology ultimately depends.

Unleashing human capital

In the traditional organization in the UK and US, the general belief is that the lower down you are in the organization, the less important your role. (The massive pay differentials between front-line employees and chief executive officers (CEOs) in Anglo-Saxon organizations is a manifestation of this belief, and the top people often openly express that they are worth the differential.) Shop-floor operatives, labourers, drivers, shop assistants, etc., are perceived as dispensable and not vital to the operation. However, the most effective ideas are only available from those employees actually doing the job, *not* from remote top management, the elite bright spark or genius. The Western notion of the 'big idea', to be handed down from the top, is a 'big mistake'. It has disempowered and demotivated the workforce, led to missed opportunities, and meant that large amounts of money have been squandered on poor investments (see also Chapter 7).

It is the knowledge and skills of all employees, working together, which is fundamental for achieving the continuous improvement in quality, efficiency and innovation necessary to compete in the global market. This will be considered from Chapter 3 onwards.

Example: Swatch   The meteoric rise in sales of Swatch[2] watches in the 1980s, following the production of a prototype in 1981, was based on the product's reasonable price, high reliability (quality), and high fun and fashion component (quality, innovation). The process had been initiated by the merging of the two major Swiss watch conglomerates, recommended by a leading management consultant in response to the industry's massive loss in market share to the Far East. The head of one of the divisions of the new company became a major driving force in the new development by creating an environment which enabled the young engineers and young marketers to come up with the new concept. Their ideas were unleashed by them being given full responsibility to come up with the proposal for a new direction, and full responsibility to develop and realize the new direction. In all other respects their environment remained very traditional and very old-fashioned. In the mid 1980s, the management consultant who had initiated the process and who was shortly to take over as the chairman and chief executive, wanted Swatch to be even bigger and pushed for investment in automated factories. This served to guarantee the high quality of the microscopic components. It also greatly reduced labour costs in the production process. However, if the process of squeezing out people goes too far, or if, as some claim, the chairman operates autocratically and disempowers decision-making below him, then the ultimate source of efficiency, quality, and particularly innovation—the cornerstone of their success—becomes undermined. This was recognized by a former employee who was part of the team which proposed a watch with a completely plastic case, instrumental to the new concept. Concerning the exit of a long list of managers since the chairman took over in the mid 1980s, he commented:

I cannot answer for the rest of the people if [they left] the company only for the feelings of fear and the mentality of [the chairman], but I am sure that has a big influence, and yes, he has a dictatorial tendency that is ... not a motivation for people who need to develop new things.

The danger in the long run is a return to reduced competitiveness against the Far East, particularly Japan, which has a strong people-centred approach to business (see later).

Example: Machines don't have ideas

According to the DTI, industry wastes around 20 per cent of its information technology spend. It is estimated that tens of millions, and perhaps hundreds of millions of pounds are being wasted on individual projects. Because of the frequency of the failures some are beginning to speak of a mysterious 'computer triangle' where millions of pounds are invested never to be seen again. It is widely recognized that the computer triangle is a management problem, and not the fault of the technology itself or any other factor.

Exercise

Organizations constantly depend upon all their employees for a multitude of responses and judgements necessary for delivering efficiency and the above routes to added-value needed for competitiveness. For example, on employees depends:

- the skill and judgement needed to apply new technology effectively;
- the ideas for making effective improvements and innovations in the product or service.

List other areas where the ideas and judgements of the employees are important in your organization (look at the above routes to added-value and efficiency to prompt if required).

High wage—high skill competitiveness

The futility of organizations in developed countries attempting to compete on the basis of product cost alone with the consequent importance put on low labour costs, and the crucial importance of workforce skills to add value, is now being recognized by an increasing number of bodies, including the CBI in Britain and the American Administration. These stress factors such as:

- The need to abandon trying to preserve low skill–low pay work.
- The capacity of people as the one factor of production that is unique to a nation's future standard of living.
- The need to invest in people's education, skills, and abilities to work together constructively as a basis for going up-market and adding value.
- The increased competitiveness of a high skill–high wage economy.

Similarly, the OECD jobs study (June 1994), while calling for greater flexibility in labour costs, saw the creation of a high skill–high wage economy as the best long-term route to prosperity and the solution to unemployment.

Example: The relative unimportance of labour costs

UK and US inward investment

Lower wage costs in Britain and America have been widely reported as being the reason why a number of European companies have moved operations to the former countries (e.g. Hoover's move from France to Scotland); or taken over a company (e.g. the BMW takeover of the Rover Group); and for the large percentage of Japanese inward investment in Britain. It would seem, therefore, to support the belief in the prime importance of low wage costs to competitiveness. It is for this reason that the present Government and certain business people oppose the Social Chapter of the Maastricht Treaty, which they fear will undermine competitiveness by increasing wage costs.

However, there are those, including the European CBI director, who point out that the absence of the Social Chapter in Britain has never been given as the sole reason for a company moving to Britain. They cite examples such as Hoover's move from Dijon to Glasgow, who gave a dozen different points that were taken into account in the move. Similarly, the takeover of Rover by BMW would have been inconceivable a few years previously—however low the labour costs— before the transformation in quality, efficiency and skill levels had occurred in that company through them adopting revolutionary working practices in collaboration with Honda. Likewise, Japanese and other Far East investors include in their reasons for investing in other countries: the quality of the infra-structure, technical background, human resource skills, accessibility of markets, and strong government support—not cheap labour.

UK investment in US

For reasons of the kind indicated in the previous paragraph, the biggest single location of UK direct investment overseas is the US, not cheap labour developing countries.

Brain power, efficiency and added-value

Traditional vs high tech?

The need to develop a high skill–high wage economy in order to compete successfully has led some people to conclude that there should be a development away from traditional, labour intensive and heavy industrial manufacturing, such as textiles, steel and engineering, towards more specialized high technology products relying on scientific discovery and a highly skilled workforce, in order to escape from the competition of the low-wage mass production economies of the developing third world. This view shows an ultimate lack of understanding of the key factors which make a company successful.

New added-value skills for 'old' industries

It is certainly true that growth in the 'new' industries, such as consumer electronics, telecommunications, data-processing, media production, and environmental and health-related sciences, has great potential for capturing future markets. But it is important to be aware that:

- The establishment of a high tech–high skill industry does not in itself guarantee competitiveness and success. The decimation of many high tech consumer electronic industries in the West by Japanese competition is testimony to that.
- It is possible for any industry to strive for increased efficiency and added-value, whether it be textile or electronic, steel or software, car manufacture or data processing, banking or biotechnology, etc.

On this basis a highly skilled workforce is essential for competitiveness in any industry, new or traditional, manufacturing or service.

Increasing competition

At the time of writing concern for overseas competition was heightened by the signing of the latest round of the General Agreement on Tariffs and Trade (GATT), a multilateral world-wide deal for reducing trade barriers. This latest agreement takes further a process of tariff (import tax) reductions begun after the Second World War, which has been gradually removing protection, opening up markets and laying companies open to global competition.

Winners and losers?

The GATT event led to further death warrants for traditional industries. For example, a City analyst at the time summed up what he believed the increased competition meant for companies by producing a list of likely 'winners' and 'losers'. (A similar 'winners–losers' list could be produced for other developed Western countries.) Included in his British 'winners' list were: pharmaceutical companies, the speciality chemical sector, the service sector industries such as financial services, the media: all of which had a good standing on world markets. Included in his 'losers' list were what he called the traditional manufacturing sectors, such as engineering, electric and electronic equipment, commodity chemical, and aerospace: sectors where British market share had been declining for many years. He foresaw a continuation of the diminution of their competitive position against much stronger firms and sectors in these areas in other countries.

Brain power for all industries

However, the above City analyst's message for traditional industries was not in fact as bleak as it first appeared, and it turned out to be directly in line with the positive 'added-value' view considered in the previous section. When pressed, the analyst maintained that the boards of directors of traditional manufacturing companies should not 'give up', but should try to adapt the skills and specialist knowledge and abilities that we do have to these areas so that we can actually compete:

We're not going to compete ultimately on the basis of cheap labour or massive-scale production ... we need to use our brains and use our knowledge base.

Example In spite of the early 1990s recession, and uncertainties about inflation, interest rates and the value of the pound, The Weir Group (a traditional heavy engineering manufacturer) came through able to compete effectively in world markets: turnover in excess of £400 million a year, exports approximately 60 per cent of turnover, China a major growth market. The importance of added-value and brain power is reflected in the fact that the chairman, Lord Weir, put concentration on specialist engineering at the top of his list of reasons for their success.

Summary

Traditional industries can be winners if they strive to add value in the ways indicated. There are such examples in the UK, but they are rare. The problem (considered in Chapter 2) is that in certain developed Western countries brains are being underused, and the skill and knowledge base, particularly in Britain and also to a certain extent America, is not being renewed and extended to the extent that it is within many of our major competitors in Europe and especially the Pacific rim countries such as Japan, Hong Kong, Singapore, Taiwan etc., (not to mention the newly developing South East Asian countries and mainland China). This is the basis of our relative uncompetitiveness.

The great emphasis and value put on education and learning in Far Eastern countries, e.g. Taiwan undertakes to invest at least 15 per cent of its national budget on education (three times that of the British figure), means that it will increasingly be not just Japan which poses the 'added-value' competitive threat to the West. As John Neill, group chief executive of Unipart, warns: 'What we now see in developing countries emerging very quickly is high technology, high quality, high productivity, and low wages'. In fact, wages in some of these countries are expected to increase rapidly and are already on a level with the West in some high tech industries. This is nothing for the West to rejoice over, however.

> The biggest threat to organizations in the West is not low wage economies but high education economies.

Learning and skill development, education and training, are therefore of vital priority for organizations and governments.

Key points
- Efficiency (cost per unit output) is a more important competitive measure than labour costs.
- Organizations in developed countries cannot compete on the basis of cost alone.
- Increasing efficiency and added-value are the only realistic routes to increased competitiveness in the global market place.
- Increasing brain power—knowledge and skills—is the major route to increased efficiency and added-value.
- Learning and skill development, education and training—the routes to increased knowledge and skills—are therefore the only routes to competitiveness.

Notes

1. When the quality of goods are on a par, such as in food retailing, companies can enhance competition by adding value to customer service, e.g. providing convenience in the form of a wide range of products, pleasant environment, eating and other facilities. The prevailing gap between rich and poor, however, has ensured a customer base unable to afford such unnecessary added-value. This has enabled certain retailers to compete by concentrating on low cost alone.
2. Quotation and information in this example from *The Business*, BBC 2, 21 July 1994. The interpretations are this author's.

Reference

Deming W.E. (1986). *Out of the Crises* (Massachusetts Institute of Technology, Centre for Advanced Engineering Study).

2 The training trap

Chapter 1 considered the reasons why, for any organization, to compete against increasing competition depends upon both efficiency and added-value; which in turn depend upon learning and skill development, education and training. This chapter will consider:

- The low priority put on knowledge and skills by British (and American) organizations compared with organizations in competitor countries
- The reasons why many employers put a low priority on knowledge, skills, and training.
- The re-enforcement of employers' negative attitudes to skills and training, by external institutions
- The costly 'training trap' that these attitudes lead to.

The anti-learning anti-training culture

There are differing views on the state of education and training in Britain. Some sing the praises of government initiatives such as the national curriculum, and the system of vocational education leading to National and General National qualifications (NVQs and GNVQs); and some point out that British manufacturers increased their spending on training and innovation during the early 1990s recession. Directly opposing this view, others strongly criticize the inadequacy of education, and the NVQ–GNVQ system; and claim that cutting back on training has been the first thing companies have done in the recession.

Whatever the exact statistics on rates of improvement and rates of spending, etc. may be, the following is certain:

- Britain has a poor skills and training record compared to many of its more successful competitor countries.
- Much of the training that takes place is wasteful and ineffective.
- Educational performance compares badly with competitor countries.

Certain aspects of the above are also true of America.

Education and training: some statistics

- Nearly two-thirds (64 per cent) of the British workforce has no kind of qualification (Green *et al.*, 1993; RSA, 1994).
- Britain spends less of its gross domestic product on training than most of its European competitors (UK 0.17 per cent, Greece 0.23 per cent, Germany 0.47 per cent: OECD figures, 1993)
- In 1993 the UK had only 250 000 people on apprenticeship schemes compared with two million in Germany (Green *et al.*, 1993). (The 1994 White Paper on Competitiveness committed funds for creating a further 30 000 places on modern apprenticeships. Although some action was taken by the Government, in 1995 the National Commission on Education criticized the fact that there was no publicly funded educational element.)
- The World Competitiveness Report 1995 incorporating the views of business and economic leaders showed:

	UK ranking out of 48 countires
Skilled human resources	24
Qualified engineers	40
Education system	35
Overall competitiveness	18

- Proportions of 16-year-olds reaching equivalent qualifications, and youth attainment of comparable 18 + qualifications (Green *et al.*, 1993), were:

	% 16-year-olds	*% 18 + -year-olds*
Germany	62	68
France	66	48
Japan	50	80
England	27	29

- In 1995 the Government was criticized by the National Commission on Education for not adopting its target of at least 90 per cent of young people to be working up to 18 for a national qualification. (Although by then 90 per cent of 16-year-olds were going on to education and training, by the age of 17 in the region of half of them were either dropping out or failing.)
- Investigation (Green *et al.*, 1993) showed how higher skill levels, e.g. in Germany, produced higher productivity linked with:
  - defects and problems being detected at an early stage;
  - machine downtime being significantly lower;
  - less wastage;
  - more flexible and rapid response to markets, e.g. changeover times (from one style to another) were around 3 days for German machinists compared to 6 weeks or more for British machinists;
  - greater variety of high quality, high value-added products;
  - ability to compete on quality not price (in contrast British producers such as furniture manufacturers competed on price rather than on quality);

– higher exports.

Britain is not alone in its poor education and training record. Although exact parallels cannot be made, there are similarities in the USA. For example, it was reported that:

- Only 8 per cent of our [US] front-line workers receive any formal training once on the job (NCEE, 1990).
- The USA has the highest public expenditure per school student and the lowest educational outcomes (Japan has the lowest public expenditure per student and the highest educational outcomes) (Green *et al.*, 1993).

Government response

In May 1994 the British Government produced a White Paper: *Competitiveness: Helping Britain to Win*, which identified Britain's acute skills shortage, and directed funds to redressing the situation. Although it was strongly criticized by opposition parties and others for not doing enough, it did indicate the Government's endorsement of the central position of education and training to competitiveness. The new American administration in 1993 took steps to redress their situation. There is recognition on both sides of the Atlantic that there is a lot of ground to be made up in order to match major competitors.

In Britain, in June 1995, the National Commission on Education, while acknowledging that some improvements had been made, expressed dismay at the extent to which Government action had lagged behind rhetoric. Its criticism related to a failure to act on key recommendations it had made 18 months earlier, such as raising basic standards, setting training targets, improving inner city education, and expanding nursery schools. The continuing concern was that unless education had a higher priority, Britain would be seriously disadvantaged against global economic competitors.

Employers' reasons for not training

Not all the employers' fault

It is unlikely that this country will do what must be done about workers' skills unless there is a strong demand from business and industry for people with those skills.

This was a comment made by Hillary Clinton in 1992. It is a valid comment which applies equally to Britain. Both in America and Britain by the mid-1990s still only a small percentage of employers have been concerned about a skills shortage, although this has begun to change. However, the judgemental 'preaching' stance against employers, often taken by those who provide training, fails to recognize that not all the blame for poor skills can be laid at the door of 'unenlightened' employers, and that Britain's poor skills and training record is part of a general *anti-learning, anti-training culture* of which those who exhort—mainly training providers and Government—have been part.

The main reasons given by employers for not training

A number of Training and Enterprise Councils (TECs) I approached did not have data on employers' reasons for not training. This is in line with the general remoteness that exists between training providers and employers (see also Chapter 8); and in the case of TECs it is reflected in Coopers and Lybrand's findings that three out of five companies said that TECs had no or very limited effect on their human resource development (CBI, 1993).

However, North Nottinghamshire TEC was able to provide relevant information. According to their Employer Survey for which they received 250 responses (TEC, 1993, pp. 34, 35):

- Fourteen per cent of firms admitted they don't train—fear of poaching cited as main reason.
- The main problems employers face in providing training for employees are:
  - giving employees time off (33 per cent);
  - meeting the cost of training (29 per cent);
  - a belief that suitable courses not available (10 per cent).

Research undertaken for the Government's Training Agency (1989) reported that companies gave the following major reasons for not training:

- They had a static or declining workforce that was already trained (51 per cent).
- They only recruited people who were already experienced (42 per cent).
- The work involved did not require skills (32 per cent).

The researchers concluded from the second reason that a considerable number of firms (approximately 8 per cent) have a deliberate policy of poaching from establishments who train.

Putting together the above reports and feedback I have received from employers, the main reasons employers give for undertaking no training or limited training are:

1 Training has no value because:
  (a) knowledge and skills are not needed;
  (b) knowledge and skill development is not needed because employees are available from the labour market/poaching;
  (c) training courses are not suitable.
2 We can't afford the time to release employees.
3 We can't afford the cost.
4 Trained employees will be poached by other companies.

For these reasons, training is generally perceived as a cost rather than an investment.

External constraints re-enforcing employers' anti-learning anti-training attitudes

The above four main reasons why employers do no or little training are in fact interlinked, and they all reflect a low value put on skills and knowledge. (A similar low value is often put on training even in those organizations that do train: see below.) However, the attitudes and concerns of employers they represent are understandable to the extent that they reflect and are re-enforced by the following external factors.

Training providers

- Traditional 'off-the-peg' courses have been too theoretical and not directly related to the workplace. (*Re-enforces 1(c) in employers*)
- Traditional courses have been inflexible and college based. (*Re-enforces 2 in employers*)

Financial institutions

- Banks, large shareholders, etc., put emphasis on short-term cash-flow considerations and short-term financial gain (annual profit, quarterly share dividend, etc.), encouraging the employer's traditional perception of training as a cost not an investment. (*Re-enforces 3, 2, and 1(a) and (b) in employers*)

Government and competitor firms

- Tax reforms introduced in the 1970s had the effect of exacerbating companies' tendency to distribute earnings in the form of dividends, rather than reinvest in such things as training and research & development (R&D). Re-enforces the short termism referred under the previous heading. (*Re-enforces 3, 2, and 1(a) and (b) in employers*)

  British firms pay out in dividends more than double the average for the rest of the world.

- There is no legal obligation for 16 to 18-year-olds who start work to undertake training, and comparatively high amounts are being paid to relatively unskilled youth workers which could be more effectively spent on training. (*Re-enforces 1(a), 1(b), 2 and 3 in employers*)

  The incentives to become skilled are low. For many low level qualifications, e.g. an NVQ 2, it is actually financially better to go and get a job at 16 than it is to go and get that qualification and then a fully paid job after the 2 years of training.

- There are no national or regional agreements for a fixed rate of pay for young trainees and for the trainee to remain with their training employer for a minimum of 4 to 5 years, e.g. as in Germany, encouraging the British trained employee to go to the highest bidder and employers not to train but to poach. (*Re-enforces 4, 3, 2 and 1(b) in employers*)

  Young British trainees are paid two-thirds of the adult skilled wage while their German counterparts are paid a third (CBI, 1993)

- There is no legal obligation for the licensing of tradesmen, as is the case for example in Germany and Australia, to prevent employment without reaching minimum standards and qualifications. This encourages cowboy operators who can set up without any qualifications, and employers to accept lower standards in employees. (*Re-enforces 1(a), 2 and 3 in employers*)

  In 1991 the Institute of Plumbing, concerned about the quality of much British plumbing, attempted to win legislative backing for the kind of registration scheme—backed by rigorous qualifications—which exists in virtually every other European country. It was blocked by the Government.

- Low school attainment, condoned by lack of licensing, encourages low standards in the workplace. It imposes considerable additional costs on responsible employers for 'remedial' education and training to bring the majority of trainees to the level of competence of those in other countries. (*Re-enforces 1(a), 2 and 3 in employers*)

- The system of vocational education (NVQs and GNVQs), brought in (1988) to help counter the low school attainment level, has been criticized in comparison with most European vocational education and training as over-bureaucratic and:
  - lacking in theory, and too narrowly based to create understanding and allow for subsequent occupational flexibility needed in the workplace (e.g. Smithers, 1993; see also Chapter 8);
  - lacking external assessment undermining credibility of qualification gained.

  This encourages employers to believe that the Government is not serious about delivering its part of the 'knowledge and skills' bargain in the way governments do in more successful competitor countries, and to see most employees as mindless 'pairs of hands'. (*Re-enforces 1a, 2 and 3 in employers*)

- The Training and Enterprise Councils (TECs), founded by the Government in 1991 to 'revolutionize' training and tackle the country's skills deficit, were immediately targeted for cut backs by the Treasury when they made a surplus of £232 million (through, they maintain, efficiency savings) during their first 2 years of operating. They have also been reported to be wasting around £250 million a year (Bennett *et al.*, 1994), and, under output-related funding pressures from Government, to be directing funds towards inadequate and inappropriate training. In 1994, the cross-party Public Accounts Committee criticized the Department of Employment for 'large amounts of doubtful and incorrect payments to training providers and to TECs'; noted subsequent moves to clarify TECs' obligations to financial controls; but also attacked other expenditure including a £48 million investment on a new computer system for TECs and £11 million on consultancies, as poor and inadequate. If the general approach is not overhauled, then it will signal to employers that the Government is not serious about the skills revolution. (*Re-enforces 1(a), 2 and 3 in employers*)

- By 1995 there were no other plans by Government to intervene to give greater incentives to train, such as bigger tax incentives; or by having training levies on firms such as in France. (*Re-enforces 1, 2 and and 3 in employers*)

The above aspects relating to training providers, investors, and Government therefore work against employers training, and re-enforce the low priority put on learning and skills development by many employers. The outcome is a general 'anti-learning, anti-training' national culture. Attitudes will need to change across the board to produce a 'support' culture, creating new government regulations and long-term 'patient' money from investors. These would transmit a message which gives priority to the value of skills for organizational success, and thereby encourage and re-enforce pro-learning and training attitudes in employers.

The training trap

The general anti-learning anti-training culture depicted above has traditionally led employers into one of two possible traps.

Trap 1: The no-training trap

Those employers and top managers who consider training costly and irrelevant are often locked into the *no-training trap* and the consequent cost to efficiency and innovation. It becomes a vicious circle. These tend to be small to medium-sized businesses, who are more likely to succumb to the external short-termist financial and other pressures indicated above (see also Chapter 7).

Trap 2: The waste-training trap

On the other hand there has been a tendency for larger employers with greater cash reserves, to succumb to the preachings and rhetoric of training providers, and to 'train for training's sake' (CBI, 1993, para 60), thereby falling into the costly and ineffective *waste-training trap*.

Send someone on a course to be trained, and note '*send*'. And then, like a shirt which has been to the laundry, they'll come back clean and neatly pressed.

Sir Adrian Cadbury

Management concentrates on inputs, such as training budgets or the time spent on training, rather than outputs. Similarly to those in the 'no-training' trap, training is perceived as a cost which is irrelevant to the actual job, and therefore inessential. This is indicated by the fact that there was a substantial decline in the proportion of medium to large establishments with a training budget between 1992 and 1993, during the recession, according to Government statistics. Also, those with high level qualifications are more likely to receive training than those with low or no qualification, and training activity tends to be highest for managers and other professionals (HMSO, 1993).

In short, even of those employers who do train, many use a 'scattergun approach', and do not consider training necessary for the majority of the workforce.

The key to escape the training trap

As certain organizations which did well during the late 1980s/early 1990s recession testified, there is one key thing which all employers can do to avoid the above training traps. This enables organizations to overcome the short-termist external constraints and the related perception of training as an irrelevant cost which work against skill development, and so greatly improve the success of their workplaces. The rest of this book will consider what that key thing is, its full benefits, and how to achieve them.

References

Bennett R.J., Wicks P. and McCoshan A. (1994). *Local Empowerment and Business Services: Britain's Experiment with Training and Enterprise Councils* (UCL Press, London).

CBI (1993). *Training: the Business Case* (Confederation of British Industry, London).

HMSO (1993). *Training Statistics 1993* (HMSO, London).

NCEE (1990). *America's Choice: High Skills or Low Wages!*, a report of the Commission on the Skills of the American Workforce (National Centre on Education and the Economy, New York).

Green A. and Steedman H. (1993). *Educational Provision, Educational Attainment and the Needs of Industry: a review of research for Germany, France, Japan, the USA and Britain* (National Institute of Economic and Social Research, London).

RSA (1994). *Tomorrow's Company: the Role of Business in a Changing World*, Interim Report (The Royal Society for the encouragement of Arts, Manufactures & Commerce, London).

Smithers A. (1993) *All Our Futures: Britain's Education Revolution*, a report of the Channel 4 Commission on Education. Produced for Channel 4 by Broadcasting Support Services in association with the Centre for Education and Employment Research, University of Manchester (Channel 4 Television, London).

TEC (1993). *North Nottinghamshire Local Economic Review 1993–94*, (North Nottinghamshire Training and Enterprise Council, Mansfield).

Training Agency (1989). *Training in Britain: a study of funding, activity and attitudes—Employers' Activities* (HMSO, London).

3 Organizational culture: from training trap to competitiveness

The 'anti-learning anti-training' culture manifested in the attitudes and practices considered in Chapter 2 has its roots in an authoritarian 'hierarchical' national culture. This is reflected in prevailing hierarchically run organizations both in the public and private sectors, and the traditional mass production working culture. In turn, at the root of this general hierarchical culture are core hierarchical attitudes and behaviours/'skills'. The central importance of core attitudes and skills both to an organization's culture and training will be considered in Chapter 4 and following chapters. First, this chapter will consider:

- The key characteristics of the traditional hierarchical working culture
- Examples indicating why and how the traditional culture needs to change to escape the training trap.

The traditional hierarchical 'mass production' working culture

By the mid-1990s, the majority of organizations in Britain, America, and certain European countries, in both the private and public sectors, still operated around hierarchical working practices. Although the term 'mass production' is usually applied to the manufacturing production line, its characteristics are essentially the same for all hierarchically run organizations.

Key characteristics: command and control

The hierarchical working culture:

- separates jobs into simple mindless, unskilled or low skill repetitive tasks
- does not expect or require (the majority of) employees to think;
- gives little or no responsibility to employees
- expects employees just to turn up on time and precisely follow instructions like robots
- pays managers—the experts, the people with the brains who know everything—to be in authority and do the thinking

- uses managers to supervise employees autocratically and dictatorially, i.e. come up with ideas, deal with problems, make the decisions, instruct, and order.

This form of work organization is often referred to as the 'Taylor' model.

Learning and training irrelevant

As the majority of employees are not required to think, to be creative, to solve problems, to take decisions, etc., there is no need for them to have knowledge about the products and processes and develop their skills. It is an 'anti-learning' culture where training, therefore, plays no part.

Hierarchical mass production successful in past

The mass production working culture was successful, especially in Britain and America, when companies were not faced with competition from other countries. It increased productivity, reduced prices, and increased sales and workers' pay.

The need for change

Over the last few decades, as foreign competition has increased, the mediocre quality of, and lack of innovation in, products of the traditional hierarchical working culture has been revealed and shown to be no match for the superior quality and innovation of countries such as former West Germany and Japan. The competition from the emerging low-cost, low-wage economies in Asia, in particular SE Asia, which have for some time overtaken the developed countries in growth league tables, has worsened the situation.

As considered in Chapter 1, to survive against stronger competition from abroad (and at home), organizations need to improve added-value and efficiency/productivity through developing and harnessing knowledge and skills. It is clear, therefore, why the traditional and still prevalent 'anti-learning' hierarchical working culture has been inadequate for this purpose. Organizations need to change, and the only way to do this effectively is in the way their more successful competitors in the developed world have been doing; and, as far as many Japanese companies are concerned, have been doing since the 1950s. The experiences of the four Western organizations considered below point the way to the key thing that needs to be done.

Exercise: four examples

Consider the four examples below in the light of the following ways used by organizations to improve competitiveness. Write down which move(s) each company found effective.

- investing in new technology/equipment
- implementing a quality system (e.g. BS 5750)
- introducing new products

- use of external consultants
- building new factories
- management training
- shop-floor training
- installing a quality control department/inspectors.

Example 1: Motorola

The problem Motorola,[1] the American electronics giant, was highly successful until overseas industries, re-built after the war, posed increased competition and wiped out entire production areas.

The response Senior managers thought they had risen to the challenge by concentrating on new products. But in a meeting in 1979 a top sales executive shocked the management when he voiced the unavoidable truth: 'Gentlemen, we have a problem. The quality of our products stinks'.

To deal with the quality problem, in the early 1980s consultants came and went. The Dean of Motorola University recollects:

We decide, oh, what we need to do is train middle managers and all the operators and key individuals are new tools of quality. We wasted $7 million on that ...

And never mistake investment in technology for salvation, thinking you eliminate the people part. What happened is the more we invested in technology the greater was our dependence on key people.

Finally, after 1985, top management became convinced that the company's future depended on a fundamental change in the traditional mass production working culture to one built around teams, relying heavily on front-line workers. Skills were suddenly vital, and the company embarked on a massive education and training programme costing $127 million by the early 1990s.

The change is simply but forcefully expressed by a Motorola supervisor:

People were used to being told what to do, it was a culture that was our culture—'you do this, you do that'—they looked for me to show up and tell them what to do. People told me what to do, I showed up in the morning and I got my orders, I got production orders—'this is what we're going to do, this is when it needs to be done'.

In the new way of working, people decide for themselves how jobs should be done; they help each other with problems, maintaining workflow; and they interchange between jobs within their teams and between departments. They have enhanced understanding of the processes, and have become comfortable with complex equipment, enabling them to pick up faults more rapidly so producing a higher quality product. And they are able to make suggestions for improving the work processes, increasing output.

The result   The corporate vice president observed how employees are now 'really excited and turned on' by their work, and so work harder. Consequently there is need for a lot fewer managers. The company considerably cut development and production time for its products, considerably reduced numbers of component parts for one of its main products, and considerably reduced product defects. They achieved a level of quality of just 3.4 defects per million by 1989, but acknowledge there is a lot more room for improvement. The gains in added-value and efficiency have meant that the company's products have been able to match Japanese and other competition.

Example 2: ILFORD

The problem   In the mid-1980s ILFORD[2] tried to produce a revolutionary new black and white film. However, they were unable to move from the development stage to full-scale production without losing quality. In their struggle they came close to saying the film was not producible and totally withdrawing it from the market.

The response   In 1985 the beginnings of a quality programme was implemented, with a Deming quality initiative, supplemented with a raft of training programmes for all managers over a short period of time. This ultimately failed to generate any significant improvement. They questioned the efficacy of putting the responsibility for quality in the hands of an inspector at the end of the production line. For example a product such as film or paper would be sent out of the production department to be checked, and accepted or rejected, by people who had not had any involvement in its manufacture. They considered whether the skills of the workforce could produce better quality than relying on inspectors. Managers believed that the knowledge and expertise needed were present within the company, but because there was no system where people could work together collaboratively within and across functions to solve the problem, the knowledge and expertise of each individual was not being effectively communicated and pooled, and it was this they believed that prevented them from finding the cause of the problem and how to solve it.

The company considered putting in a quality system, such as BS 5750, to draw on the untapped expertise, and convert it into a written standard procedure. They rapidly realized, however, that this was not going to solve their problem because such a system would not address critical business issues relating to what you are getting out of your workforce, whether they are being more productive, and whether you are satisfying the customers' needs.

The Board decided to adopt a different approach, focusing more on organizational change. The 'people-focus' in the journey to quality became more prominent through a major change programme begun in 1989, when the company was acquired by a large US-owned chemical company. A reduction in the number of layers of the hierarchy and grades took place, and the bonus system rewarding output only was removed. Teamworking was developed at all levels in the organization. Seven years after the problem of the unproducible film, the head of Human Resources recounted how the change involved management's realization that 'the way forward was to look at the whole way we manage our people, we motivate them, and we involve them'. Employees, including shop-floor workers, were expected and allowed to become involved in decision-making and problem-solving, and were given the responsibility for quality. An employee contrasts the situation with the past, where people were in effect expected 'to leave their brains in the locker', and just to go on to the shop-floor and do the job. There was considerable investment in training, moves to further harmonization, and well-developed employee involvement schemes.

The management style emphasized teamwork, cooperation and openness, and corporate principles include 'employee development' and 'the encouragement of participation'. The change process itself was built around involvement and communication.

The result   Labour relations have been transformed and a new awareness of production processes has been created. Management observes how shop-floor workers are more satisfied and motivated, and produce less waste. The approach to training and its evaluation has fundamentally changed, and now involves a two-way agreement between line manager and employee, facilitating relevant, continuous and cost-effective training and development. The company has won a number of prestigious awards since 1991, quality is up, production costs are down, there has been expansion into the Japanese market, and profit has increased enabling greatly increased investment even through the recession.

Example 3: United Aluminium

The problem   United Aluminium[3] of Connecticut invested heavily in new technology to increase productivity. In the subsequent 6 years up to 1991 the productivity of their rolling mills had grown at just 0.5 per cent a year.

The response   To attempt to remedy the situation, the company brought together management, mill operators and other factory staff into a single project team. The vice president recounted how he and other managers got together with the operators and talked to them: 'What do you think is possible if we eliminated all of the barriers, what could you guys do, what would be a reasonable step up of your performance?' The number they came out with was 15 per cent, and so management responded: 'Well look, why don't we shoot for the goal, let's make 15 per cent our target in 8 weeks, OK? No more than 8 weeks, no fancy changes, we're not going to be making any other major changes in terms of equipment and what not, just with what we've got. Let's see what we can do'.

Once the figure of a 15 per cent jump in mill productivity had been agreed, the team made a list of all the things that stood in the way of achieving the improvement. They then worked through the list questioning everything from maintenance procedures to the way raw materials were handled. One by one the obstacles were removed.

The result   The team in fact achieved a 17 per cent improvement in productivity in 8 weeks. The vice president observed: 'when you realize that over the previous 6 years we had only gotten about 0.5 per cent improvement per year, this was an enormous step up in performance'.

Example 4: Xerox

The problem   In the early 1980s, after a decade of increasing costs and declining market share, Xerox[4] was jolted out of what it now refers to as its 'overly bureaucratic' and 'complacent' 'internal arrogance', by the greatly superior performance of its Japanese competitors. Senior management suddenly realized that their nearest Japanese competitor was able to sell products at approximately Xerox's cost of building them i.e. about half Xerox's selling price, and still make good profits. They also gave the customer a choice and did not arrogantly ignore customer needs. Behind this massive difference in performance were facts such as the company had nine times more suppliers, it was rejecting ten times as many machines on the production line, and it took twice as long to get its product to market.[5] As a consequence corporate profits plummeted from $1.149 billion in 1980 to $600 million in 1981. In the words of Rank Xerox chief executive Bernard Fournier, 'We discovered that Japanese competition was able to completely eat businesses ... looking at the penetration of our market we discovered that we would have been the next one on the list to disappear'.

The response   In order to understand the competition, the then CEO David Kearns travelled many times to Japan, as did company engineers, to find out about the Japanese way of working. In response, in 1983, the company established its 'Leadership through Quality' programme. The first step was to create, and communicate to every employee, a quality policy equating 'quality' with innovative products and services that fully satisfy (external and internal) customer requirements; and to specify that quality is the job of every employee. The second step in 1984 was to develop and begin a training programme of a minimum of 3 days for every employee, on how to use formal quality processes and tools.

From their observation of the Japanese competition they learned that 'employee [and supplier] involvement and participative problem solving are absolutely essential for improving quality'. At the heart of the changes they began to instigate, therefore, was 'changing the management philosophy and the organizational structure'. They recognized the need to change from a hierarchical, functional command and control organization to a more horizontal, cross-functional, team organization, where the manager's role changes from controlling, planning and telling to one of teaching, coaching, and facilitating. This they realized would enable an environment where every employee can focus on the customer and be responsible for quality within self-managed work groups.

Their change in management philosophy was influential in the way they implemented the quality training programme. It was conducted in family groups, *starting with* the CEO and his direct reports, cascading down from the top. The training was aimed at 'empowering employees, vesting them with authority over day-to-day work decisions, and enabling them to seek and practice quality improvement in everyday activities in their job environments' (but see Chapter 11). The goal was that 'Quality should be "in the line ... by the line"', something which they claim large training departments cannot aspire to and thus are expensive and ineffective.

The result The bureaucracy, functional conflict (between Sales, Marketing, Manufacturing, Service, Personnel and Finance), and over-resourcing and inflexibility present in the previous hierarchical structure, started to be eroded. A 'significant benefit' gained was that employees grew and developed within teams, particularly those that had people from other departments, with different knowledge and skills. Motivation was increased at every level.

'Bottom-line' outcomes included: a 50 per cent reduction in materials inventory; a reduction in manufacturing supplier base from 5000 to just over 400 companies over a 5-year period; a 46 per cent reduction in production lead times; an 80 per cent reduction in raw material stocks; a 99 per cent reduction in component defects since 1984. The company continued to lose market share until 1986. After then, assisted also by the imposition of anti-dumping duties on Japanese imports, they held, and in some instances recovered market share. Rank Xerox, for example, despite tough trading conditions across Europe, achieved a 160 million ECU profit in 1992 when some competitors reported substantial losses.

Lessons to be learned: culture is key

Motorola The example shows that motivation, learning, quality, innovation and efficiency were previously blocked by a hierarchical mass production working culture. It took Japanese competition to shock top management into realizing they needed to change working practices to give all employees responsibility to meet and exceed customers' needs.

Moral New products, external consultants, investment in technology and training will not deliver the efficiency and added-value needed for competitiveness. These moves represent expensive wastes and are only likely to maximize cost-effectiveness within a working culture which fully involves employees.

ILFORD   The example shows that existing workforce skills and knowledge were not being pooled and harnessed to the full to overcome quality problems until top management supported moves to develop a more horizontal culture which involves all employees. It was not training which brought about the improved culture, but the new culture which brought about improved, more cost-effective, relevant training.

Moral Management training, quality control departments and inspectors, and quality systems, e.g. BS 5750, will not improve performance. They represent a great deal of wasted time and money.

United Aluminium   Only when top management became involved in changing working practices to fully involve the workforce in the decision-making process was full skill and equipment potential realized, and the block on productivity removed.

Moral Expenditure on expensive equipment, new factories and training will not improve productivity within a hierarchical working culture. At best it will only bring about very small improvements in performance, and it represents a great deal of wasted time and expense.

Xerox   The example illustrates that their previous highly hierarchical, bureaucratic organizational structure had created a disregard of the customer, and inflexibility and cross functional conflict, underusing and limiting workforce skills, and thereby constraining efficiency, quality and innovation. This was a situation not perceived to be a problem by top management until forced to by greatly superior Japanese performance, from whom they learned the lesson of the fundamental importance of a flexible team culture facilitating employee involvement.

Moral Policy statements and 'task-orientated' quality training programmes, will not improve competitiveness without a fundamental shift from a vertical to a more horizontal organizational structure which involves employees through a teamworking culture.

The cultural prerequisite of competitiveness   These four organizations have different products, and different people, yet the move, supported by top management, to change from the traditional hierarchical culture to begin to develop a working culture which involves all employees, has been equally vital to all of them. It is this one factor to which they each owe their great improvement in performance and competitiveness.

No quick fix At the time of writing none of these organizations have completed the culture change process, as they themselves would recognize. Changing the working culture cannot be a quick fix, and it is not achievable by having a 3-day training course. For instance, at Xerox it took about 4 years for their development to begin to improve market share (see also Chapter 11). Similarly, at ILFORD in the year following the introduction of their quality programme in 1985, an ACAS survey indicated that many managers were seen as remote, arrogant and autocratic, despite rhetoric on openness, teamwork and employee development and participation. In 1991 the general response was that recent years had seen a change to a more open style, exemplified by more senior management interaction with employees, but the process is not yet complete, as considered in Chapter 5.

In both Britain and America organizations that were changing their culture, such as the above examples, were still in the minority in the first half of the 1990s, and the traditional 'anti-learning' hierarchical culture prevailed.

Training no good in itself The four examples show that the following ways which organizations often use to improve performance (also listed at the start of the exercise) do not, in themselves, improve performance and competitiveness:

- new technology/equipment—*no good in itself*
- quality systems (e.g. BS 5750)—*no good*
- new products—*no good in itself*
- external consultants—*no good in itself*
- building new factories—*no good in itself*
- middle management training—*no good in itself*
- shop-floor training—*no good in itself*
- quality control department/inspectors—*no good*

The key lesson The main lesson to be learned is that improving performance to the level needed to match increasing competition, cannot be achieved through any particular task-orientated training programme, quality system, or piece of machinery, etc. An organization must:

- begin to change from the traditional hierarchical culture to a culture of team involvement, which
  - fully involves and empowers front-line employees;
  - requires and enables learning and skill development.

Training is a cultural issue

If organizations take heed of the importance of culture, they can save themselves a great deal of time and money.

The 'new' collaborative 'team production' working culture

This directly contrasts with the traditional hierarchical 'mass production' working culture outlined above.

Key characteristics: coach and facilitate

The collaborative working culture:

- does not separate out simple repetitive tasks: employees are involved together in all aspects of the job (multiskilling)
- expects and pays (all) employees—who do the work and often know best what needs to be done—to think
- gives responsibility for quality to all, including front-line employees;
- enables and motivates employees continuously to learn, make decisions, solve problems and innovate
- uses managers as coaches to facilitate the intelligence, creativity, knowledge and skills of employees.

Learning and training central

As all workers are required to think, be creative, solve problems, take decisions, etc., knowledge and skills are central to this 'collaborative' workplace. It is a 'learning' culture, therefore, where skill development and training are highly valued.

Collaborative team production the only basis for long-term success

The increased capacity and flexibility of employees which genuine team production enables is essential for increasing efficiency, quality, innovation and, therefore, competitiveness. For example:

- It enables people to fully participate and to help each other to come up with ideas for solving problems, maintaining the workflow.
- It promotes and enables multiskilling as people interchange within and between teams and departments.
- It enables people to stand in for others when they are away, maintaining the workflow.
- It enables employees to cope better with change, responding faster to the customers' needs and fluctuation in demand.
- Most importantly, it motivates the workforce to be creative and do a quality job.

Summary

The traditional hierarchical 'mass production' working culture is an anti-learning anti-training culture. It does not require or enable high levels of knowledge and skills in the majority of employees. This, however, as was considered in Chapter 1, is central for achieving the levels of efficiency and added-value needed to match and survive rapidly increasing competition. The most effective thing that organizations can do to increase their competitiveness, therefore, is to escape the training trap—of either ignoring skill development and training, or wastefully throwing money at ineffective training and development (mainly for the highly qualified, managers, etc.), new equipment and quality systems—by changing from the traditional hierarchical working culture to a 'team production' culture which fully involves, utilizes and extends every employee.

Notes

1. Quotations and information from: *Total Quality: Time to Take Off the Rose-tinted Spectacles*, the results of a survey conducted by A.T. Kearney in association with the *TQM Magazine*, 1991; *The Money Programme*, BBC 2, 17 January 1993. The interpretations are this author's.

2. Quotations and information from: *New Developments in Employee Involvement*, by Mick Marchington, John Goodman, Adrian Wilkinson and Peter Ackers, UMIST, Department of Employment, May 1992; *Quality: People Management Matters*, Institute of Personnel Management, 1993; *Business Matters*, BBC 2, 29 July 1993; interview with Frank Sharp, H.R. Director ILFORD, December 1993. The interpretations are this author's.

3. Quotations and information from: *Business Matters*, BBC 2, 5 August 1993. The interpretations are this author's.

4. Quotations and information from: *Total Quality: Transforming the Company Seminar*, background reading, Rank Xerox UK March 1993; 'The Rank Xerox Quality Journey', *European Quality*, June 1993; *In Business*, BBC Radio 4, 31 March 1993. The interpretations are this author's.

5. Rank Xerox have pointed out that another factor which contributed to the price difference was unfair 'dumping' of Japanese-built machines into the European market-place. "After lengthy review the EU has decided to continue until October 1997 anti-dumping duties imposed by the EU in 1987 and to impose for the first time (from October 1995) anti-dumping duties on high volume light-lens copiers."

4 A collaborative working culture: key to continuous learning and cost-effective training

Chapter 3 looked at the need for organizations to change from the prevailing traditional hierarchical culture to a collaborative team culture in order to escape the 'no-training' or 'waste-training' traps which undermine the ability of organizations to match and survive increasing competition in the global market-place. The present chapter will:

- Attack the idea of the new 'knowledge worker', and re-enforce the importance of working culture
- Start to indicate how to develop a teamworking culture by identifying traditionally neglected core attitudes and skills, and show them to be essential for:
  - a *genuine* team culture
  - continuous *cost-free* learning and skill development
  - cost-effective training

Myth of the 'new' knowledge worker

Since the early 1990s it has become fashionable to claim that 'knowledge workers' will increasingly need to take over in organizations in the future. A major reason given is that manual (particularly unskilled) workers are being, and will continue to be, squeezed out by new technology and cheaper labour abroad. Certainly, as considered in Chapter 1, technological advance has meant that organizations need to invest in increasingly complex high tech equipment in order, if nothing else, to keep up with the efficiency and added-value gains this equipment allows. Therefore workers will need the technical knowledge and skills to operate this equipment. Also workers will need appropriate high tech knowledge and skills in order to work in the increasing number of new industries manufacturing high tech products, whether consumer products or equipment for industry.

But the tendency to class shop-floor workers in traditional industries as 'manual' and those in the new industries as 'professional', and only to class professional workers and managerial workers as 'knowledge workers', is mistaken. Similarly, it gives a misleading picture to say, as one reporter did, 'In the past there were plenty of decent jobs around where education didn't much matter'; or as another said, there is now a 'rise in the value of knowledge'.

Knowledge and skills for all

> Knowledge and technical skills are important for competitiveness, even for 'manual' workers in traditional industries such as motorcycle manufacture, car manufacture, and shipbuilding.

This is not because of a recent need to use new complex high tech equipment in these traditional industries in order to keep up with the efficiency and added-value gains this equipment enables, but because knowledge and skills in traditional 'manual' workers has always been important for high efficiency, product quality and innovation. It has been the relatively low level of knowledge and skills in British workers, and certain other western countries such as America, and a corresponding underinvestment in technology compared to their Japanese counterparts in particular, which have been major reasons for the uncompetitiveness and decline of many traditional industries in these countries since the 1960s (e.g. Example 1, Chapter 7). (The reason has not been purely because Japanese industry has been more automated. True, they did rapidly automate from the late 1960s, but since that time and up until the 1990s Japanese car firms, for example, have been less automated than in the West.[1])

Concerning the need for knowledge workers, Peter Wickens, former personnel director of Nissan U.K., has maintained:

... towards the end of this century *every* worker will need to be a knowledge worker. Knowledge is not going to be reserved for people in managerial or professional positions. All people must be able positively to contribute because that is where success will come from.[2]

That, of course, is what the Japanese have realized for many decades.

Knowledge and technical skills not enough

Knowledge and technical skills in workers is a necessary ingredient for competitiveness, but it is not sufficient. As the examples in Chapter 3 indicated, in addition, organizations need to have a *collaborative team culture*. We saw, for example, in the United Aluminium case, how the knowledge and skills of the shop-floor workers only became fully utilized through a team approach which equally involved them with management in problem-solving and decision-making relating to work processes, and removing the barriers that existed in the previous top-down hierarchical culture. Only in this way was every employee enabled and motivated to do a good job and work to their full potential.

**Example:
'knowledge workers'
not enough**

Having a company where the majority of employees are 'knowledge workers' is not sufficient therefore to guarantee success against strong competition. The culture has to be right to enable their full contribution. This is illustrated by the Financial and Accountancy Service Industries. For example, I was asked by a management consultant who worked for a leading London-based accountancy firm whether my writings relating to organizational culture would help the company's particular problem of losing young trainees once they had become qualified. A year or two previously in the depths of the early 1990s recession, the media reported widely on the redundancies being made by leading accountancy firms. Young employees who had only been employed for a few years were reported to be shocked at being made redundant. The lack of commitment shown to employees is a characteristic of the traditional hierarchical culture, and results in a reciprocal lack of commitment by employees (see Chapter 6). The outcome is a great deal of money wasted on training. As long as all accountancy firms operate hierarchically there is no competitive threat, but such inefficiency would not go unpenalized against a collaboratively run competitor.

*'Hire and fire' culture
undermines knowledge
and performance*

Some weeks after writing the above paragraph, it was echoed in a report produced by the London Human Resource Group.[3] The report condemned the 'hire and fire' culture displayed by City institutions in response to the first real recession in the financial sector that occurred in the early 1990s. The report's author saw this reflection of the predominant approach in manufacturing as highly damaging to what had been up to then the City's long-competitive advantage over its rivals in other countries. He found widespread misunderstandings and staff very cynical about the future, which was reducing productivity and performance. Consequently he predicted that job-centred cost-cutting, without giving thought to the 'livewood' which is being cut into, would mean that the industry would go into decline relative to other financial centres, in the same way as manufacturing had. Although, he claimed, the City had something like three to five years' lead in terms of its pool of know-how, other centres were catching up: they were finding out about what kind of skills are needed, what kinds of knowledge, and recruiting people from the City, a process that was likely to increase when the recession ended in mainland Europe. In line with the points being made in this section he summarized:

The City has got very vital know-how, it has got its vital staff ... the skills, it has got good players, but it doesn't really know how to get the best out of them. And the reason for that is that it is still applying the old bureaucratic rules in management practices, while expecting the deployment of skills to produce very high performance.

Key 'added-value' team skills

In addition to the full utilization of the technical skills and knowledge of employees, a team approach is essential for the effective acquisition of new knowledge and skills. The reason for this, as will be considered below and in subsequent chapters, is that team skills are inextricably linked with effective learning, both in the workplace and in formal education and training. Also, as will be considered below, it is the learning and motivation which a team approach enables that form the *mainspring* of quality, innovation, service, etc., that is, added-value and efficiency, needed for competitiveness and success.

Team culture and competitiveness

Only those companies which develop a genuine team culture will succeed against strong competition, where every employee is a 'knowledge worker', and where the distinction between professional and manual, manager and employee, merges. Again, the Japanese example illustrates the point. Teamwork and general employee involvement in the decisions that affect their work has been a characteristic of their major organizations for over four decades. There is not the strict division between worker and manager, or between supplier and customer, as there is in the traditional hierarchical western culture, but a more collaborative approach. This aspect, often marginalized in the West, is the key to their competitive edge.

Transferable 'thinking' skills

Within the 'new' team culture, employees, therefore, will be required and encouraged to develop not just the knowledge and technical skills relating to a particular area of work, but also a broad set of 'interaction' skills, sometimes referred to as 'thinking' skills, relating to problem-solving and decision-making. These will be considered fully below. They are the foundation of understanding, multiskilling, application, transferability, adaptation, etc., and will be, as they always have been, required for people to operate to their full potential. The prevalent view today, which sees training in terms of the need to learn either specific management skills, or specific technical skills to do a particular job of work or to be able to use high tech equipment effectively, is therefore too narrow. It misses out the key team-learning skills necessary for continuous knowledge and skill development, and the general effectiveness of all employees.

Recognition for core skills

The need for these team interaction skills is recognized by an increasing number of people. For example, top management at one successful company, has talked of the need for everybody in business to be part of a 'self-managing team' which requires 'a vast array of totally new skills' not expected previously at shop-floor level.

German industrialists responsible for vocational training refer to the inadequacy of workers knowing only a specific job, and the need for them to be able to interchange flexibly between jobs, including team leadership, by being multiskilled. The American National Center on

Education and the Economy's Commission on skills points out the need to allow front-line workers to use judgement and make decisions, and give them more responsibility for a wide range of tasks previously done by others from quality control to production scheduling in order to achieve high performance. Finally, the situation is well expressed by an American trade union official responsible for apprentice training when he says: 'we've come to realize that critical thinking skills are very very important because the worker is now into lifelong learning. If you take a narrow approach they are only going to learn their job. We want them to be able to learn the jobs of tomorrow and we don't even know what they are yet. A person who has critical thinking skills will be able to develop workplans, study skills, etc., so that they can learn those jobs with the minimum amount of instruction.'

Collaborative team skills

The skills of collaborative teamwork are inextricably linked with effective learning and training. Before looking at this link, it is useful to consider what comprises the skills of genuine teamwork. In the West these skills are generally marginalized by managers, trainers and consultants. Even where there are genuine intentions to move beyond the teamwork-quality rhetoric which is now rife, they are often not based on a full consideration of the core skills needed, and their vital link with culture and learning.

Genuine teamwork

The word 'collaborative' is used to distinguish *genuine* teamwork from what might pass as teamwork in some organizations. Hierarchical cultures can have a team structure in place, but the 'teams' will reflect the organizational hierarchy and be based on unequal, power-based relationships which are diametrically opposed to equal, reciprocal or collaborative relationships characteristic of a genuine team. The following are just some of the different characteristics:

Collaborative team	*Hierarchical 'team'*
members given equal value/status	members not given equal value
members have equal say	dominated by minority/team leader
informal	formal
task-centred objectives	personal objectives
conflict of ideas	personal conflict
comfortable, relaxed	stiff, hostile
clarity of purpose	confusion
enjoyable	tense, fearful
enthusiasm	resentment, boredom
pleasant	nasty, aggressive
cooperative	competitive
harmonious	adversarial, confrontational
supportive	individualistic
group commitment, loyalty	self-interest

The effect of a truly collaborative team culture is summed up by the president of Nissan USA: *Employees are happy in this culture, they enjoy being here, they don't hate coming to work.*

This factor is often trivialized and sometimes ridiculed by Anglo-Saxon managers. In doing so, however, they make a profound mistake, and miss its fundamental relevance to motivation, learning, and in turn added-value and competitiveness, as will be considered below.

The broad collaborative team skills

Within a collaborative team the following broad skills are truly and fully facilitated among team members:

- discussion and communication skills
- problem-solving skills
- decision-making skills
- self–team development skills

Stated in this way they are very general and vague, and they do not inform people exactly *how* to perform these skills or what they actually need to *do* to develop them. These broad team skills are in fact interdependent and interrelated, and there is a common thread of underlying *functional skills* which each requires if they are to be undertaken effectively.

The collaborative functional skills behind the broad team skills

These include the ability to:

- initiate
- consult
- revise
- express/describe/clarify
- request/seek information
- request advice
- link
- seek and elicit alternative views, suggestions, solutions
- critically question and give feedback
- receive open critical questioning and feedback
- give alternative ideas and suggestions
- weigh up (evaluate) differing viewpoints, ideas, evidence
- inform/present
- support and develop
- plan
- delegate
- produce to plan
- infer and test (evaluate) outcomes
- promote

This list of functional skills comes closer than the above broad skills list to indicating what people need to do to operate effectively in a team. But again they do not inform people exactly *how* to perform these skills and what they actually need to do to develop them. As is the case for the broad collaborative team skills, these functional skills are interdependent and interrelated, each requiring a common core of underlying *interpersonal skills* to be undertaken effectively.

The collaborative interpersonal skills behind the functional skills

These include the following:

- listening
- openness
- non-abrasiveness
- non-judgemental
- tolerance (of differing/opposing ideas and mistakes)
- genuineness
- consistency
- objective rationality
- self-reflection/appraisal

These skills bring us closer again to what people need to do to operate effectively in a team, but once again they do not indicate exactly *how* to perform these skills, and therefore what people actually need to do to develop them. For example, it is one thing to say 'I need to listen', but another thing to do it. The important question is how can people improve and develop these core collaborative team skills? As for the previous levels of skills, these core skills are interdependent and interrelated, and ultimately their effective development requires the development of underlying core *interpersonal attitudes*, i.e. attitudes towards others and oneself.

The collaborative interpersonal attitudes/values behind the core interpersonal skills

These include the following:

- respect
- trust
- honesty
- humility
- fairness
- justice
- empathy
- liking of people

Again, as for the previous lists, these attitudes are interdependent and interrelated. Also, the separation between the collaborative attitudes and skills is not clear cut, and the distinction made is not meant to be definitive. It draws attention, however, to the importance of underlying attitudes and values.

These core attitudes bring us yet closer to indicating how people need to operate to work effectively in a team, but listing them, just as listing the skills, does not indicate what people actually need to do in practice to develop them. Changing attitudes can be difficult and takes time, which is why it takes time to develop a genuine team culture, but it is far from impossible. There are aids and procedures which can be used on a day-to-day basis in the workplace to help develop the core collaborative attitudes, and related core skills, on which everything else depends (see Chapter 10).

If the core collaborative attitudes and skills are not developed, therefore, genuine teamwork is blocked, and also effective learning and training, as will be considered in the next section. Trainers, therefore, need to be aware of the ultimate importance of these core attitudes and skills (Figure 4.1).

Broad team skills

discussion/communication, problem solving,
decision making, self-team development

↑

Functional skills

initiating, consulting, informing/presenting, supporting, requesting/
seeking (information, advice), eliciting, critical questioning and
feedback, receiving critical questioning and feedback, evaluating,
revising, linking, suggesting, expressing/describing/clarifying,
planning, inferring, delegating, producing, promoting, etc.

↑

Collaborative interpersonal skills

listening, openness, non-abrasiveness, non-judgemental tolerance,
genuineness, consistency, objective rationality, self reflection/
appraisal, etc.

↑

Collaborative interpersonal attitudes

respect, trust, honesty, humility, fairness, justice, empathy, liking of
people, etc

Figure 4.1 *Genuine teamwork—the attitudes behind the skills behind the skills*

The common skills of teamwork and learning

The previous section indicated how collaborative interpersonal skills, and underlying attitudes, are the core skills of effective teamwork. Looking through the lists above, it will be evident that the team skills (discussion and communication, problem-solving, etc.), and the functional and interpersonal skills on which they depend (the ability to critically question, evaluate evidence, present reasoned argument, listen, be open, self-reflect etc.), are also the skills of effective learning and self-directed learning.

Learning skills and added-value

The overlapping of team skills with learning skills is the basis of findings built up over many decades in both industry and education, which indicate that group participation is linked with enhanced learning and efficiency (see Jones, 1992).

> The more people participate in dialogue and the decision-making process, the more effectively they work and learn.

It is the above listed team-learning skills which a genuine team approach rests on and facilitates, which are essential for enabling employees to:

1 Fully and effectively apply their knowledge and skills in the workplace.
2 Effectively learn new knowledge and skills.
3 Form a close 'collaborative' relationship with customers and suppliers, on which a great deal of efficiency and added-value hinges (see below).

These overlap, e.g. 3 is one basis for 2 and 1. These team-learning skills, therefore, provide the *foundation* for the high levels of quality, service, innovation (i.e. added-value) and efficiency, that are necessary to compete and survive.

Culture of involvement for motivation and added-value

As well as facilitating team-learning skills, indicated earlier to be the major foundation for added-value and efficiency, the latter is also enhanced by a team culture through:

- Involvement of every employee, which means that ideas for improvement (whether in product, service, or process) can be harnessed from the whole workforce and not just a few managers.
- Involvement of front-line people, which gives better ideas for improvement because they are the ones who know the job best.
- Involvement of front-line people, giving them the respect and trust, etc. to solve problems and take decisions, and enabling them to form a close productive relationship with the supplier or customer by:
  - empowering them to use their knowledge and skills fully, and take action, speedily and effectively to meet the needs of the supplier or customer (see Milliken and Rank Xerox examples below);
  - encouraging and inculcating in them the core collaborative attitudes and skills of respect, trust, listening, openness, etc., which enables them to operate cooperatively and ethically with the customer and supplier (see examples below); and to create a

climate of trust, facilitating the development of the same core attitudes and skills in the supplier or customer, as a basis for learning from them and with them in a long-term partnership of continuous mutual improvement in product and service.

> The fashionable call for a 'learning relationship' with customers—seeking and responding to customer feedback—is only achievable by organizations developing an internal learning culture.

- The involvement process itself, where employees are shown respect, trust, listened to, etc., which enhances their self-esteem and highly *motivates* them to:
  - apply their knowledge and skills effectively and efficiently;
  - find out more about the product, service, and processes, and seek and learn new knowledge and skills;
  - deliver quality;
  - come up with ideas for improvement.

It is a powerful virtuous circle (Figure 4.2).

> The learning skills and motivation which a team culture enables, form the mainspring of innovation, quality and efficiency

Cost-free motivation, improved industrial relations, and training

A reviewer who was looking at two books, one from the UK and the other from Germany, which considered the issue of continuing vocational training, commented:

employee motivation, adaptability and improvements in industrial relations ... provide the rationale for training investment in many companies.

If this is so it is a very expensive way of improving motivation and industrial relations. Not only that, it is likely to be ineffective and therefore wasteful. It suggests an underlying hierarchical culture in those companies, in contrast to a collaborative team culture which continuously enhances motivation and improved industrial relations without expense, and uses the training budget solely for skill and knowledge development. Using training to boost motivation and improve industrial relations might have a positive short-term effect, but in the long-term these will be undermined by the underlying hierarchical culture.

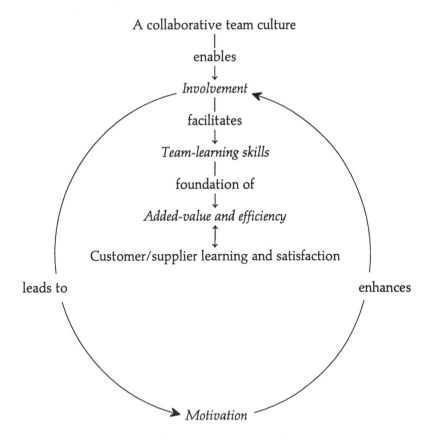

Figure 4.2 *Motivating involvement—a virtuous circle*

Culture of continuous learning and cost-effective training

When the workplace is structured around genuine flexible teams, therefore, the following situation holds:

- Every employee is enabled and motivated to fully apply and extend their knowledge and skills. This creates a culture of continuous *cost-free* learning and development.
- Priority is given to further extending knowledge and skills through *relevant* training. This is necessary for achieving cost-effective training.
- Ideas, knowledge and skills gained in courses are fully tapped and further extended and developed in the workplace by the trainee employee being fully involved in the decision-making process, fully empowered (and required—see below) to produce quality goods or services, and fully recognized for doing so. This is necessary for cost-effective training.

> Organizations will only be able continuously to tap and extend the skills of employees, and fully gain from training, within a collaborative working culture

Customer care and cost-effective training

Knowledge of the product, cited in Chapter 1 as an added-value factor, is essential for providing a speedy, quality service and other aspects of added-value for the customer. Earlier it was considered how a team culture which centres on relationships of respect, trust, honesty, etc., not only ensures employee learning and knowledge of the product through involvement and relevant training, but also ensures closeness to the customer by empowering, encouraging, and requiring employees to fully use their knowledge and skills to meet the needs of the customer. In a company culture which does not nurture the latter, training is rendered ineffective and wasteful.

Example

Failing to meet the needs of the customer, and its links with training, is illustrated in the case of the Financial Services industry. The poor treatment of customers who were given bad advice by financial salespeople (and advisors) and persuaded to buy inappropriate products (personal pensions, insurance products, etc.), which did not meet their needs, ultimately led to regulatory fines amounting to millions of pounds being imposed on some of the major insurance companies. This mis-selling also led to the possibility of hundreds of millions of pounds of compensation being paid to customers, widespread undermining of public confidence and trust in the industry, and moves by the industry to improve training.

A factor jeopardizing the quality of service to the customer was the salesforce's inadequate knowledge of products available, linked with no or inadequate training. In 1992 the industry regulator, LAUTRO, began to introduce some training standards for the industry. Leaving aside the controversy over the adequacy of these standards, there was a yet more fundamental concern recognized by some commentators.

> Training and knowledge of the product, although necessary, are not sufficient for delivering customer satisfaction.

That is, no matter how good the training, and how knowledgeable the salespeople, it will still not guarantee that they behave ethically in the best interests of the customer, especially when the commission system of payment has been shown to put a high risk on people being sold products which generate greatest commission rather than ones that suit their particular needs. The problem did not arise, however, solely from slack, dishonest and greedy salespeople. The quality of advice given is ultimately dependent on the culture of the industry. The commission-based system of payment, the requirement that sales staff meet a target of sales to keep their job, and the fact that managements knew and seemingly accepted that salespeople were selling inappropriate products accruing greatest commission, give a strong message of what that culture has been. However much money is spent in future on training to improve quality of service—whether it is on increasing knowledge of product, quality or customer care—it will be largely money down the drain unless the culture issue is addressed.

The industry's culture of disinterest in the consumer was revealed by the regulator's (Securities and Investment Board) move in 1995 to introduce rules forcing companies to be open about commissions and charges generally. These rules of disclosure were thought likely to do more than any of the other measures that had been introduced to empower and protect the customer. They immediately started to drive down profit margins in the industry, and began to force companies to reassess their product structures to offer better value for the customer. However, the disclosure rules do not *guarantee* that a person will not be sold a poor or an inappropriate product. Ultimately this requires a culture change.

Cascading poor treatment and ineffective training

The example illustrates the general point made in Chapter 3, and earlier in this chapter, that training in knowledge and skills is no good in itself for achieving the added-value necessary for long-term competitiveness. If consumers' interests are to be safeguarded, there needs to be a root and branch culture change in companies which gives priority to senior and middle managers forming a collaborative relationship with employees based on respect, openness, honesty, trust, listening, etc. This would require a structure which rewards managers on these criteria, rather than other factors such as short-term numerical goals (see Chapters 6 and 12); in the case of the Financial Services industry, for example, meeting a certain target of sales. Only this will remove the pressure from middle managers and front-line staff, and enable continuous learning, cost-effective training, and a corresponding collaborative relationship with customers, as a basis for satisfying the latter's needs. In short, no amount of training will overcome the knock-on effect of poor hierarchical treatment: from managers to employees, and employees to customers.

> Cost-effective training is dependent on forming long-term collaborative relationships with customers, which is dependent on forming long-term collaborative relationships with employees.

> Collaborative relationships with customers are the key to success through repeat business and reputation.

Supplier partnership and cost-effective training

Similarly, a company culture which does not nurture a close mutually beneficial collaborative relationship with its suppliers undermines its training. The traditional Anglo-Saxon organization has had an arm's-length, short-term, confrontational relationship with its suppliers, 'shopping around' a large supplier base, often setting one against the other, and beating prices down as low as possible. This is illustrated by the 'blind bidding' systems used by UK and US car manufacturers. General Motors (GM), for example, introduced a programme of centralized purchasing to reduce component prices, in their moves to meet the challenge of Japanese competition. Suppliers were not involved in the concept and planning stages, and previously used suppliers were brought under pressure to rebid for the work at much lower prices. This created a climate of distrust and secrecy, and typically suppliers withheld information from their customer in order to strengthen their negotiating position, and some bid below cost. As a result some efficient suppliers lost work to less efficient and less qualified suppliers who bid at a lower cost. Although the exercise was reported to have produced impressive savings, it was not without problems in the long term. GM encountered quality problems and delivery problems, and was forced to bring some of the work back to some of the efficient suppliers at extra costs. This illustrates that:

> However good the training might be to improve efficiency, quality and innovation, it will be undermined in the traditional organization by the nature of the relationship with the supplier.

The above short-term adversarial customer–supplier relationship contrasts with those formed by Japanese companies which are characterized by a long-term collaborative approach and have been a major basis for Japanese companies' increases in efficiency, quality and technological innovation (e.g. Example 1, Chapter 7). Some UK and US companies are moving in this direction under the influence of Japanese 'transplants'. Also, some large-scale food and DIY retailers are beginning to build partnerships with suppliers. They aim to have a closer more open relationship with fewer suppliers, enabling forward planning, greater economies of scale, investment in new plant and equipment, and just-in-time distribution, as a basis for efficiency gains and cost-cutting.

Genuine versus superficial partnership

However, the following difference between the motivation of Japanese and many UK and US companies for developing a partnership approach with suppliers suggests that the move by UK companies is not being accompanied by the correct attitudinal changes needed to reap the full benefits of mutual efficiency, learning and innovation.

Superficial motivation: the profit motive

The main reason why many UK and US companies are only now making moves to develop less adversarial partnerships with suppliers is to cut costs. Against the pressure of low inflation, increasing global competition, and a limit to the amount a company can cut costs by downsizing, some companies see this as the only way left open to them to make a further drive for increasing profits.

Genuine motivation: serving customers

A long-term collaborative relationship with suppliers has been a cornerstone of Japanese companies' endeavour to add value while keeping costs low or reducing costs, increasing customer satisfaction and market share. The traditionally different perspective and psychology of the Japanese compared with most British and American companies is encapsulated in the following comment:

> American companies find it difficult to understand that price is of little consideration in an attempt to open up negotiations with Japanese firms. More important than price in the Japanese way of doing business is continual improvement of quality, which can be achieved only on a long-term relationship of loyalty and trust, foreign to the American way of doing business. (Deming, 1986, p.43)

Without the development of core attitudes such as respect, trust and honesty, UK and US companies will not create reciprocal respect, trust and honesty in suppliers. Entrenched in the old confrontational approaches, suppliers justifiably will be cynical of the genuineness of the customer company's intention to develop a truly open and mutually beneficial partnership. This undermines investment and commitment. Potential gains will only be maximized when attitudes (and related skills) change from top management levels, and this will not occur overnight.

Traditional hierarchical organizations which have put greatest store on cost-cutting and short-term gain, therefore, at the expense of respectful, trusting, open, long-term relationships with suppliers, have undermined quality and service, and lost full efficiency and technology advancements, thereby undermining any training undertaken by employees, however relevant and effective that training might otherwise have been.

Quality of product or service ultimately depends on the quality of relationships.

> Training is rendered ineffective and wasteful in a company culture which does not nurture long-term collaborative relationships with its employees, customers and suppliers, based on respect, openness, trust and honesty, etc.

Examples of skill/knowledge utilization and continuous learning in developing team cultures

Each of the following examples illustrates how respecting and trusting employees to come up with ideas and solutions, requires, enables and motivates them to utilize fully their knowledge and skills, and also to find out more about their job and their products and to extend their knowledge and skills.

Milliken Industrials

At Milliken Industrials,[4] through involvement and being empowered to make their own decisions, the production workers have become eager to contribute towards the company's success. They take a keen interest in customers and suppliers. One example, in the European branch of this American textile group based in Wigan, involved a problem where they were producing off-quality products due to poor raw material coming into one of the UK plants. The production team arranged a meeting with the operators on the supplier's shop-floor. No management were present. The result was an 80 per cent improvement in quality in the next delivery, with further improvements ever since. The managing director dryly observed: 'In the old days, our management, talking to our supplier's management, could have successfully kept the problem going for years!'. To match the involvement allowed to employees, the company 'do a great deal of education and training'. Through genuine employee involvement, the company greatly improved performance. At the European branch 90 per cent of product quality problems were eliminated, lead times reduced to 20 per cent of what they thought possible, and talk of 10-fold improvements was no longer met with disbelief. In 1993 the European branch won first place in the European Quality Award.

Motorola

A shop-floor team used to have to lift the heavy components they were building on and off the production line which was originally designed by plant engineers. Injuries were common. With the help of an industrial engineer who provided the basics in engineering information, the team designed a new production line, and came up with a simple lifting device. This has prevented back strain and enabled higher output.

Rank Xerox   Developing skills and knowledge of the product in sales and service employees has been a cornerstone of Rank Xerox's[5] success in improving quality of service and customer satisfaction. To this end, in order to keep the skills and knowledge base abreast of new product development, a vast amount of their millions of dollars spent on training is invested in service and sales education. A major factor in delivering quality of service, however, has been the empowerment of staff closest to the customer to fully use their knowledge and skills, by being given the responsibility to solve problems and make decisions, without the need for them to seek authority through a chain of command. For example, a customer service engineer has the power to abort a machine install if conditions are not satisfactory. A service manager can decide to replace any customer's machine that is not performing to standard. This greatly speeds up the process of fixing any problems, in turn greatly enhancing customer satisfaction.

Small business example: Jardinerie   Involving and empowering employees has been a central philosophy of the Jardinerie[6] chain of garden centres from its beginnings in 1984. The company grew rapidly and by 1990 had six garden centres and an interior landscaping business. The then managing director, and later chairman, was anxious that their team approach should not be lost as they grew to a larger organization which demanded new company structures and systems. Consequently, he made what was from their point of view the 'big move' of instigating a training and development programme with an external consultant, to ensure that staff were involved in the change process. The training, a 5-day course, began with directors and senior managers. It encouraged them to question their own assumptions (see Chapter 12), and consider the way they were perceived by others. It was considered by senior managers to have generally improved their perceptions of staff potential and the value of staff ideas. After further training workshops for the staff, a mixed team toured the company to initiate improvement project teams, explaining they were about fully using people's talents and skills, and giving all staff a chance to grow and develop. Instead of imposing top down, all employees had opportunities to come up with ideas for projects. These were then grouped under headings such as 'Customer care', 'Communications', and 'Wastage', and project teams of between four and eight people from different functions were set up on a voluntary basis around these areas. The teams were self-managed and members shared responsibility for planning and implementing project work.

In 1995 the number of people involved in project teams continued to spread through the workforce of about 300 people, and a culture was being created where people use this approach as part of their normal day. Problems were being solved as the teams came up with ideas, and more efficient and simple systems and practices were being put into place. As the company continued to expand, the plans were to evolve an increasingly decentralized structure.

**Small business
example: Seabait**

Genuine team effort and continuous learning have been the driving force behind Seabait,[7] a company on the Northumberland coast, pioneering the farming of ragworms, bait for coarse fishing. Begun as a two-man band in 1985 (the managing and research directors), the company employed about 24 people by 1995. The commitment to a team approach by the managing and research directors was put to the test during their first year of production when 80 per cent of the ragworm stock died. No employee was laid off despite great financial difficulties, indicating the extent to which value was put on the contribution of all employees, from the school leavers who originally joined on a Youth Training Scheme (YTS) all the way through to managing director. This attitude was repaid by a reciprocal commitment of the workforce. During the difficult time, they all bought shares in the company to raise new money, and they have since shown high motivation and commitment to learning and improvement at all levels. For example, as the company began to overcome their original teething problems in design and operation procedures, one employee, who began on a YTS, talked enthusiastically about making improvements and understanding more about looking after the worms. The extent of his learning and the company's ability to utilize it is shown by the fact that 4 years later he became the assistant manager of the farm.

In-house training and development through self-generated ideas and assessment has been at the heart of their learning process. Benefits cited were an increase in productivity, decrease in waste, reduction in disease, and a happier and more motivated environment. The learning process was enhanced by a mutually beneficial partnership with Newcastle University, incorporating parallel research and staff–student interchange. In contrast to the prevailing tendency to under-use and waste the human resource, Seabait has shown a rare ability to use it fully to maximize efficiency, quality and innovation. By 1995 this had led to numerous first placings in awards for innovation, small business enterprise, environmental achievement (including the Queen's Award) and training; and plans for continued future expansion.

Steelcase

In the early 1990s Steelcase,[8] a worldwide maker of office furniture based in Michigan, began to reap the benefits of a programme begun in 1987 to involve all its (tens of thousands of) employees in the decision-making process. The belief was that only in this way could the company create the level of quality and service needed to survive. Teams began to be developed throughout the organization, which was generally welcomed by employees.

I think [the team system] gives employees a lot more confidence and a lot more ownership of their job. I feel better about my job knowing that I have some say in what's going on. You're not just walking in and doing your job and walking out. You go home and you think about something that's gone on at work where before you didn't really do that. Or you think about your team, what they're doing, you think about them while you're doing your job during the day, and that's different, to actually think about the decisions that are going on. (*Shop-floor employee*).

We made a management presentation ... we had to go through and find facts and figures on why this would be a good move. We made a flow chart, and showed them exactly how our product runs now and how it will run if we have this move ... and what kind of cost savings it would make. (*Shop-floor employee*)

The management listened, agreed and gave the go ahead. There began to be a continuously increasing payback in terms of morale, commitment, savings (amounting to millions of dollars), quality and service.

Varian Oncology Systems

Taken over in the mid 1980s, Varian Oncology Systems,[9] a 126-employee UK-based subsidiary of the American medical manufacturer Varian Associates Inc., began to develop a structure of self-managed teams encouraging every employee to participate.

I've been in engineering since I left school, and I was always told what machine I could go on, how I should work it. This is the first time ever that I've told the management what machine I would like and how I would like to work it. (*Shop-floor employee*)

We've gone out and bought this machine. We decided on the actual machine, the size and everything, told them the bottom line of how much it was going to cost, and they said 'Yes, go ahead and get it'. I mean, I've never worked in a place like that before. (*Shop-floor employee*)

We've to see for ourselves what job we need to do next, and pick up whichever one is required and just do that job. We're our own bosses really. (*Shop-floor employee*)

The departmental and cross-functional teams are involved in improving production processes, solving *ad hoc* problems, or developing particular projects. The benefits have been in terms of increased morale, commitment and employee orientation to the company; and the managing director points out a 'quite dramatic' financial impact through, for example, reduced cycle times, increased stock turns, and reduced defects, improving performance by 15 per cent per annum over the first 9 years, and maintaining this despite the vagaries of the international market. Within the 9 years the team approach has been operative, the company has won awards for innovation, technological achievement, the Queen's awards for Export and Technology, the National Training award; and it has been a finalist in the European Quality Award.

Summary

A genuine 'collaborative' team culture, and the team-learning skills it facilitates, has the following benefits:

- It empowers and motivates all employees to fully utilize their abilities, knowledge and skills.

- It encourages continuous cost-free learning and skill development in the workplace, motivating every employee to find out more about and improve products, processes and service.
- It facilitates close and productive relationships between employees, customers and suppliers.
- It puts financial priority on improving the knowledge and skills of all employees through training.
- It enables cost-effective training by:
  - endeavouring to make training relevant to the needs of the employee's job;
  - enabling employees to fully utilize, experiment with, and fully extend their newly learned knowledge and skills back in the workplace.

None of these benefits is possible in the traditional hierarchical culture, and therefore neither is the high value-added and efficiency which they give rise to. The contrast with the traditional hierarchical culture is an aspect included in Chapter 5, which looks at the key factor for achieving a genuine team culture, and the implication for trainers.

Exercise   To increase your awareness of the use of the team-learning skills given above, observe the use or lack of them, and the core interpersonal attitudes and skills which underlie them, in your organization. In your judgement to what extent do you think the team-learning skills are genuinely operative, and to what extent do you think there is 'hierarchical' teamwork, in the following situations:

- Interaction within senior management?
- Interaction between senior management and middle management?
- Interaction within middle management?
- Interaction between middle management and the shop-floor?
- Interaction between senior management and the shop-floor?

How do you think the team-learning skills could be improved in these interactions? Whose responsibility is it?

Notes   1. From private communication with Professor Daniel Jones, co-author of *The Machine that Changed the World*, Macmillan, London, 1990.
2. Based on private communication with Peter Wickens, 1995.
3. The quotation and information in the ensuing paragraph is from a Radio 4 interview (10 February, 1994), with Professor Amin Rajan, author of *Winning People*, London Human Resource Group.
4. Based on the transcript of a talk given by Clive Jeanes, Managing Director of Milliken UK, to an Economist Conference on Empowerment, 1993.
5. Based on: interview with a training manager, Rank Xerox UK, July 1994; *Total Quality: Transforming the Company Seminar*, background reading, Rank Xerox UK, March 1993.

6. From private communication with Ken Allen, Jardinerie Chairman, and John Teire, Charlebury Consultants, Gloucestershire, June 1995.
7. Based on private communications with Peter Cowin, Managing Director, June 1995.
8. Quotations transcribed from *Business Matters*, BBC 2, 8 August 1991.
9. Based on private communications with John Peel, Managing Director, April, June 1995; quotations transcribed from *Winning*, BBC 1, 31 October 1993.

Reference

Deming W.E. (1986). *Out of the Crises* (Massachusetts Institute of Technology, Centre for Advanced Engineering Study).

Jones S. (1992). *The Human Factor: Maximizing Team Efficiency Through Collaborative Leadership* (Kogan Page, London).

5 Priorities for trainers 1: top management commitment to culture change

Chapter 4 identified core attitudes and skills common to effective learning and teamwork, and considered how a genuine team culture enables both continuous 'cost-free' learning/skill development in the workplace, and cost-effective training. This chapter will consider:

- Why developing genuine team organizational culture requires the active commitment of the top manager
- How a top manager with hierarchical attitudes and 'skills' blocks the skills route to high efficiency and added-value
- The need for trainers not to underestimate the key influence of the top manager, and collaborative skills development, on learning and training

The key role of the top manager

Manager as coach

To achieve continuous workplace learning and cost-effective training in the way indicated in Chapter 4, every employee will need to be *genuinely* empowered to interact in teams in the ways listed (summarized in Figure 4.1), and allowed to act on decisions and *make mistakes*. If this is not allowed then the learning process will not get off the ground, and people's skill development will be stunted.

The only way people will genuinely be empowered to work and learn in teams, therefore, is if the team leader (say shop-floor supervisor) enables true participation or collaboration, by allowing and encouraging e.g.

- team reflection on work issues
- open critical questioning and feedback
- suggestion of new ideas and solutions

- decision-making
- action
- evaluation of ideas and outcomes
- risk-taking and mistakes.

The role of the team leader would then be one of colleague, coaching team members, encouraging and helping them to learn and perform better, learning from them and with them, and generally facilitating an efficient mutually supportive community, within their teams, with other teams, and with customers and suppliers.

The common skills of teamwork, learning and leadership

The above will only occur, however, if the team leader has and/or is developing the core collaborative skills and underlying attitudes, i.e.:

- *respect* for employees and their knowledge and skill potential
- *trust* in employees and their abilities
- *humility* (absence of arrogance) about one's own knowledge and skills etc.

as the basis for:

- an ability to encourage (e.g. by open questioning, Chapter 10), and *listen* to employees' views, ideas and suggestions
- an ability to be *open* with employees
- an ability to take open feedback and criticism from employees
- an ability to avoid personally *judging* employees and to be *tolerant* of differing and opposing views
- an ability to avoid personally judging and to be tolerant of people's mistakes etc.

These abilities are closely linked, as will be considered in Chapter 12. The core attitudes and skills are essential for facilitating the involvement of team members. In other words, unless a team leader has (or is developing) these core attitudes and skills, he or she will block off involvement and therefore the development of these attitudes and skills, and the learning they enable, in team members. In short, they will be a poor leader. They would also, of course, block off their own learning.

> The core attitudes and skills of leadership are one and the same as the core attitudes and skills of effective teamwork and learning.

Cascading the learning culture

In turn, the only way the team leader will be able to effectively and fully develop and deploy the core collaborative attitudes and skills necessary for effective teamwork and learning, is if he or she is enabled to participate in a *genuine* team approach with their next in line—say departmental manager—and so on to the very top manager (CEO). There will in fact need to be a culture of equal teams right throughout an organization enabling learning, and this will only occur if the top manager has or is developing the core collaborative interpersonal skills and underlying attitudes (Figure 5.1).

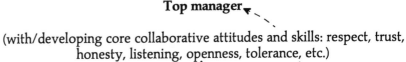

Top manager

(with/developing core collaborative attitudes and skills: respect, trust, honesty, listening, openness, tolerance, etc.)

Senior managers

Department managers

Supervisors

Employees

A flexible, equal-footing, 'horizontal' culture, where ideas, learning and decisions for action, are empowered from the 'bottom' up, through:
⟷ collaborative, two-way dialogue in interchanging teams
⟵ - ➤ two-way interaction (possibly in teams)

Figure 5.1   *Cascading the learning culture*

Example   Key collaborative attitudes of respect for and trust in people and their abilities are prerequisites of genuine team involvement. Invariably, those companies which have or are in the process of developing a team culture, have a top manager who, to a greater or lesser extent, exhibits these basic attitudes towards the value of people. The respect and trust needed is well illustrated in the following comment by the Managing Director of Varian Oncology Systems[1] referred to in Chapter 4.

The key is empowering the teams to deal with their projects, to deal with their budgets on a daily basis without reference really to upper management in the traditional sense. So once they've been given their brief, once they have formed their mission statements for themselves, then you let them go. And this is absolutely vital, they *have to* be let go. By all means supervise, but do not interfere.

Collaborative attitudes (respect, trust, etc.) and related skills are absolutely vital for this viewpoint, and the subsequent genuine empowerment of employees exemplified at the end of Chapter 4.

Top management influence on learning and training

A collaborative top manager will ensure continuous learning and cost-effective training by:

- re-enforcing and breeding collaborative team-learning attitudes and skills down the line
- further facilitating team leaders' development of the correct attitudes and skills by instigating a horizontal organizational structure (see Chapter 6)
- further ensuring the development of the correct attitudes and skills through training (see Chapter 12)
- endeavouring to link training courses with the needs of the workplace by developing training needs assessment (see Chapter 7)
- giving priority of funding to training, R&D and equipment (see Chapter 7).

Traditional top management and the anti-learning culture

Core hierarchical 'skills' and ineffective leadership

In contrast to the above learning culture, the traditional hierarchical working culture centres on interpersonal attitudes and 'skills' which diametrically oppose the core collaborative attitudes and skills (Figure 5.2). As in the case for the core collaborative attitudes and skills, these hierarchical attitudes and skills are interdependent and overlapping.

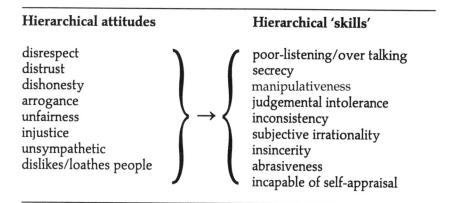

Hierarchical attitudes	Hierarchical 'skills'
disrespect	poor-listening/over talking
distrust	secrecy
dishonesty	manipulativeness
arrogance	judgemental intolerance
unfairness	inconsistency
injustice	subjective irrationality
unsympathetic	insincerity
dislikes/loathes people	abrasiveness
	incapable of self-appraisal

Figure 5.2 *Hierarchical attitudes and 'skills'*

In the traditional culture managers generally make it difficult for anyone else below them in the hierarchy to implement new and better strategies and practices. Underlying this is the lack of respect for employees, a distrust in their abilities, an inflated and arrogant view of their own abilities, etc., which makes them, for example, unable to listen, judgemental, intolerant of opposing views and mistakes, secretive. He or she, therefore:

- blocks open discussion
- blocks enquiry/critical questioning
- blocks alternative ideas and suggestions
- blocks evaluation, etc.

In other words, a manager with hierarchical attitudes and 'skills', blocks the collaborative interactions of group discussion, problem-solving and decision-making etc., and thereby blocks the learning process in subordinates. Instead of being enabled to develop the core learning attitudes and skills considered above, 'team' members are more likely to develop the 'anti-learning' hierarchical attitudes and 'skills' modelled and imposed by the 'team' leader. (See Chapter 6 for a consideration of the fear-power factor behind middle managers' behaviour in the traditional culture.)

Example: The collaborative learning—hierarchical anti-learning contrast

A 4-year project (Chaney and Teel, 1977) to train supervisors to employ a participative group approach in a large manufacturing company led among other things to the following findings.

1 'Successful supervisors' showed genuine interest in employee ideas and feelings, encouraged an open, supportive atmosphere, listened attentively to employees without making snap judgements, openly acted to implement employees' suggestions giving feedback. *Outcome*: significant productivity gains in the employee group.

2 'Unsuccessful supervisors' showed insincerity and an inability to listen to employees, they 'went through the motions' of asking for employee comments and suggestions but did not pay much attention to them. *Outcome*: a cynicism and lack of cooperativeness by employees; the quick realization that they were part of an artificial exercise; the offering of only superficial or negative comments.

Cascading the anti-learning culture

A top manager who has core hierarchical attitudes and skills will re-enforce and breed these in his or her senior management, and so on down the line. They will cascade down through an organization, producing a rigid hierarchical and bureaucratic culture, blocking the collaborative interactions of consultation, open discussion, critical evaluation, group decision-making, etc., in turn blocking the full utilization of employees' knowledge and skills, continuous 'on-the-job' learning and skill development, and cost-effective training, enabled by a collaborative approach (Figure 5.3).

Example: the anti-learning cascade

A team leader at the Rover Car plant in Cowley reminisces:[2]

Life has changed a lot. A few years ago they (supervisors) used to be very aggressive, and I think that was because their managers were aggressive and their managers' managers were aggressive, and that obviously used to feed down on to the shop-floor.

The same point is made by the supervisor in the Motorola example considered in Chapter 3, when he refers to the way 'telling people what to do' was passed down the line in the old culture.

Top manager

(with core hierarchical attitudes and skills: disrespect, mistrust, dishonesty, inability to listen, secrecy, etc.)

↓

Senior managers

↓

Department managers

↓

Supervisors

↓

Employees

A rigid, unequal, 'vertical' culture, where ideas and learning are blocked through:
→ hierarchical one-way monologue where orders, proposals, ideas, decisions, etc. are imposed from the top.

Figure 5.3 *Cascading the anti-learning culture*

In contrast to a collaborative culture, therefore, people do not relate on an equal-footing basis in teams either within or across departments. If there is some kind of team structure, it will be a facade and based on non-cooperative, adversarial interactions ultimately controlled from the top.

Hierarchical top management and the training trap

At the root of the low value put on learning and skill development by the traditional hierarchical culture referred to in Chapter 3 is a lack of the collaborative attitudes of respect and trust etc., bred from the top. As considered in Chapter 2, such a culture is likely to be caught in either the 'no-training' trap or the costly 'waste-training' trap. There are two ways in which the traditional organization brings about wasteful training.

1 The low value put on learning and skill development, despite rhetoric to the contrary, means that little to no endeavour is made to link training with the needs of the workplace, and consequently employees tend to be sent away on irrelevant courses.

2 Even if a training course used is directly relevant to the workplace, then it will be undermined when the employees return to the same rigid working culture:
   (a) In the case of leadership-team skills courses, employees will have to put aside their newly gained knowledge and skills to resume the old ways of working, as decisions and strategies are set by people up the line and the 'team' approach is a facade and hoax.
   (b) In the case of technical skills training, the traditional hierarchical working culture—blocking questions, consultation, evaluation, etc. and involvement in decisions for action—prevents employees from fully using and extending their newly gained knowledge and skills, in turn blocking innovation, efficiency and quality.

In both cases training will not be fully effective, it will represent wasted time and money, and it is likely to create cynicism and demotivation. The extent to which this culture factor has traditionally undermined cost-effective training in British companies is revealed in the following understatement in a CBI report, at the end of a section on evaluating training effectiveness:

It is equally important that wherever possible employers allow people the opportunity to apply the lessons learned from training. (CBI, 1993, para. 80)

The underestimated influence of the top manager

Although, as considered in Chapter 2, the external constraints of an anti-learning, anti-training national culture re-enforce and encourage anti-learning anti-training attitudes in employers, examples of successful organizations indicate that strong collaborative attitudes at the very top of an organization can overcome such constraints. (That is not to deny, however, that it is not such an easy job to invest long-term in employees in Britain and certain other Western countries, as it is in many countries in the Far East, Germany and Sweden, etc., where there is more external support.) Also, as has been considered, investment in people does not always mean *financial* expenditure on training, and those smaller organizations which perhaps feel the squeeze of external factors to a greater extent, can, cost-free, greatly gain in performance through the continuous learning and skill development enabled by a collaborative team approach in the workplace.

The far-reaching influence of the top manager is often underestimated, perhaps not so much in small organizations, but certainly in middle and large size organizations. There is the belief that what goes on in individual departments or on the shop-floor has some kind of autonomy of its own: how, after all, can the way people operate and interact on the shop-floor or in any particular office have anything to do with the way people interact in the boardroom, especially if that boardroom is in a different location or different country? People talk about culture as though it is the product of the various employees and departments. There is often a belief that middle managers, training managers, quality managers, departmental managers, etc. have complete autonomy to influence what occurs. Linked with this belief there is the tendency for individual employees to allocate sole responsibility or blame for a particular situation, or procedure, or rule, to one's immediate line manager or departmental manager (and vice versa). These beliefs are mistaken as they overlook the unbroken and unbreakable chain of interactions which permeate down from the top, and through which the attitudes and skills of the top person cascade and strongly influence others. Also, it is not only that people will feel pressured to act in certain ways to please those above for fear of reprisal or job loss, but they will feel pressured (consciously or unconsciously) to take on the characteristics of the culture of the organization, and their attitudes and skills (and related behaviour) will begin to reflect those set at the top. Only the strongest minded will be able to resist, and most people will be influenced in some way.

> People are pressured consciously or unconsciously to take on attitudes and behaviours set by the top manager (CEO).

Kaizen and top management commitment
The key role of top management in culture change is humorously but effectively expressed in the following comment by Masaaki Imal of the Kaizen Institute (Kaizen simply means continual improvement, however small, by involving everybody in an organization):

There are three most important words to make Kaizen work. Those are first, senior management commitment; second, senior management commitment; third, senior management commitment.

In the examples considered in Chapter 3 for instance—ILFORD, Motorola, Xerox and United Aluminium—it was in each case top management's realization of the need for change, and their active involvement in starting to bring about that change, which initiated the culture change process. (Significantly, the inception of major changes at ILFORD coincided with a change in ownership and the managing director.) The contrasting outcomes of hierarchical and collaborative top managers is summarized in Figure 5.4.

Summary
The continuous learning and cost-effective training required for maximizing added-value and efficiency, hinges on:

- Top manager commitment to collaborative culture development.

This in turn hinges on him or her developing:

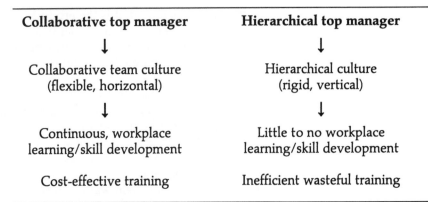

Collaborative top manager	Hierarchical top manager
↓	↓
Collaborative team culture (flexible, horizontal)	Hierarchical culture (rigid, vertical)
↓	↓
Continuous, workplace learning/skill development	Little to no workplace learning/skill development
Cost-effective training	Inefficient wasteful training

Figure 5.4 *Key role of the top manager (CEO) in culture, learning and training*

● Core collaborative 'soft' interpersonal attitudes and skills.

These two factors therefore underpin the key role of training and human resource managers.

> A major priority for training and HR managers is to gain the active commitment of the top manager to developing core 'collaborative' attitudes and skills, as the basis for developing a learning culture (Figure 5.5; see Chapter 6).

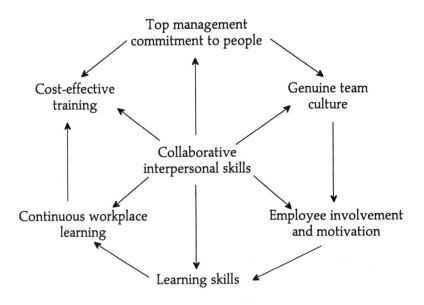

Figure 5.5 *The central importance of interpersonal skills from the top for developing a learning culture*

Notes

1. See note 9, Chapter 4.
2. Quotation transcribed from *High Interest*, Channel 4 Television, 23 January 1994.

References

CBI (1993). *Training: the Business Case* (Confederation of British Industry, London).

Chaney F.B and Teel K.S. (1977). 'Participative Management: a practical experience', in F.J. Bridges and G.E. Chapman (eds), *Critical Incidents in Organizational Behaviour and Administration*, pp.225–230 (Prentice-Hall, Englewood Cliffs, NJ).

6 Priorities for trainers 2: overcoming barriers through structural changes

Chapter 5 considered the key role of the top manager in culture, learning and training. This chapter will build on Chapter 5 by considering

- Barriers to developing a learning team culture encountered by trainers
- The structural changes a top manager with *genuine* commitment to culture change will make to overcome these barriers
- A summary of how training and HR managers can go about gaining top management commitment to culture change/a learning culture.

Widespread neglect of the culture issue

Neglect of the central importance of collaborative interpersonal attitudes and skills to an organization's culture, and of the vital link between top management, culture, learning and training, is widespread. It stems from deep-seated hierarchical attitudes which:

- scorn 'soft' interpersonal attitudes and skills, such as respect, trust, listening, openness, sincerity, and prevent people from realizing their direct relevance to performance and the bottom line
- champion a 'hard-headed', ruthless, de-humanized management approach centred on short-term accounts, costs and profit.

While many Japanese and certain Western companies have outperformed others by effectively and harmoniously harnessing the human resource for a number of decades, generations of managers, consultants and academics in the UK and US have marginalized the relevance of the horizontal 'collaborative' culture these companies nurture, and the core interpersonal attitudes and skills that underpin it.

Performance through people not systems	Trainers should be aware that it has been the neglect of the core soft skills, and the consequent inability to convert from the traditional hierarchical 'command and control' culture to a collaborative learning culture, which is at the root of the reported high failure rate of quality programmes such as TQM, and human resource management (HRM) teamwork and employee involvement techniques, such as team briefing, newsletters, suggestion schemes, quality control circles, etc.
Add-on forms of control	A hierarchical top manager often pays lip-service to these programmes and techniques but he or she creates a culture where they are deployed as 'add-ons', leaving the underlying power-based relationships and structures in tact. In fact, traditional management often uses so-called 'employee involvement' and other quality techniques and systems to enhance their own control rather than empower stakeholders. Significantly, of the techniques which mostly cater for one-way, top-down communication, team briefing was reported to have increased markedly and newsletters to have become a little more widespread, between 1984 and 1990 (Millward, 1994, p.127). In contrast, in companies where top management has or is developing core attitudes and skills of respect, trust, listening, etc., quality programmes and HR techniques become a key and integral component of a collaborative, two-way 'reciprocal' organizational culture.

The rhetoric–action gap

There has been a great deal of talk about the importance of employee learning and empowerment, but the prevailing organizational culture re-enforced by traditional structures which employ, assess and promote on the basis of criteria other than employee involvement and development, has worked against the rhetoric. This is illustrated in the case of downsizing.

Downsizing versus learning and training

The use of 'downsizing' (plant closures and job cuts), has been widely used by British and American companies up against recession and global competition, to cut costs and increase profitability. The practice is a manifestation of the low value put on people and skills in the traditional hierarchical organization. It directly contrasts with Japanese enterprises which make every effort to retain their employees even when business is bad. Job security and commitment are key factors boosting their learning, productivity and innovation, and are the basis of their continued competitiveness. The power of the hierarchical mindset in British and American companies is reflected in the use of 'delayering'—reducing the number of management layers—as a further means of cost-cutting, rather than primarily as a culture move which would safeguard jobs (see later).

Although downsizing has a short-term benefit to cash flow and the bottom line, it also has negative anti-learning effects which eat into the long-term profitability and viability of a company.

- It loses the skills of the people who leave.
- It wastes the training which those people may have undertaken.
- For the remaining workforce it creates increased workloads, insecurity, fear of job loss, and a cynicism and belief that they are just a dispensable statistic. This undermines morale, commitment and loyalty, with detrimental effects on learning, training and innovation.
- It risks losing highly skilled people dissatisfied with the job-cutting culture.
- It risks wasting very expensive training, coaching and recruitment spent on such employees.
- It loses trainees/apprentices representing a future skill loss to the company.

Undermined commitment and learning

Supervisors, middle managers and employees become cynical and uncooperative as they receive conflicting and disingenuous messages from the top, and performance generally begins to fall. Add to this the considerable time and money that is often spent on introducing quality programmes and HR techniques, involving consultancy and training, then it represents a highly wasteful and counterproductive situation.

Even those organizations where there has been some successful team development, and employees are now more involved and listened to, leading to a positive effect on performance, the extent of that positive effect will be influenced by the extent to which employees have an influence over decisions and actions. If teams down the line are, at any time, liable to receive top-down, cost-dominated decisions on budgets, job numbers, etc., without being heard and involved through a process of consultation and dialogue, then this mitigation of empowerment and autonomy will be matched by a lessening of commitment, learning and skill development (see e.g. ILFORD example below).

> Quality programmes, systems and HR techniques depend on people, and will only work within a culture which mobilizes involvement, commitment and learning.

Constraints on trainers in the traditional culture

Underestimation of the influence of the attitudes and skills of the top manager to an organization's culture, referred to in the previous chapter, is matched by a corresponding overestimation of what people down the line can achieve. The fact is that those people responsible for training and human resource development have an uphill struggle in the traditional hierarchical culture. As was mentioned earlier, there is a block on continuous on-the-job learning and cost-effective training, and this is manifested in the following hurdles for trainers.

Employer resistance to training and a learning culture

Manifestations of this resistance in traditional organizations include:

- *A resistance to funding training and development* Stemming from the top manager, there is opposition to putting funds in the direction of (relevant) training and development, and to making supportive structural changes (see below).
- *Flexible labour practices* This is often associated with the above manifestation, and is not to be confused with task and skill flexibility. There has been an emergence of the employer-led concepts of a 'flexible labour market' and 'employability'. In theory, these refer to a contract where employees accept less job security in return for opportunities from employers to develop new knowledge, skills, and expertise, as a basis for securing future employment. In practice, many employers have failed to deliver their side of the contract, and 'flexibility' has come to mean the freedom of employers to hire and fire employees if and when they please, and to create part-time and temporary (low-paid, low-skilled) work. This growing trend of employers greatly undermines employee security and commitment, and works against the capacity of an organization to tap and build on employee knowledge and expertise. It is of concern when otherwise enlightened inquiries into the role of business[1] appear to accept the principle of a flexible labour market and the encroachment of less job security (albeit within a supportive organizational and governmental framework). The move is in the opposite direction to successful learning organizations which pivot on job security and commitment (see Nissan and Rover examples below), and even opposes some Government thinking:

    We see reflected in our economic policy a keen determination .. that the recovery is sustained, that greater job security is the outcome, that higher standards of living can be delivered ...

    Economic Secretary for The Treasury, 1994

Middle management resistance to training and a learning culture

Resistance of middle managers and supervisors to culture change is reported as a common problem. The blame is usually put on them. In fact many of the reasons for this resistance stem from the inability of top management to convert their rhetoric and aspirations into action (see for example previous paragraph). The main difficulties middle managers have in going from 'cop' to 'coach' include:

- Their own embedded hierarchical attitudes which create:
  - a fear of loss of power, authority and control over subordinates whose abilities they arrogantly do not respect or trust;
  - a fear of being shown up by competent subordinates, and of losing control if, say, they openly admit they need help to understand or do something - created by a lack of humility and trust in the humility and non-judgemental tolerance of subordinates
- Ingrained hierarchical attitudes in the top manager which create:

- a fear of reprisal (job loss or blocked promotion), if they openly admit they need help to do or understand something - created by a distrust in the humility and non-judgemental tolerance of their managers;
- lack of training in the key collaborative team leadership skills;
- performance assessment on criteria other than involving and developing employees, making it difficult for them to see its relevance;
- a difficulty in reconciling the need to be more open, trusting and listening to their staff, while at the same time their own managers are unsupportive (judgemental, secretive, etc.) and create a barrier of mistrust by not communicating with or listening to them, but instead autocratically imposing orders;
- a difficulty of winning the hearts and minds of their team, and building up trust and long-term commitment to corporate goals, when there are conflicting messages from the top on the 'hire and fire' approach to organizational restructuring, creating a climate of insecurity;
- fear of job loss or blocked promotion prospects if numbers in the hierarchy are reduced (delayering), creating:
  (a) low morale, lack of commitment and loyalty
  (b) disaffection and cynicism, which undermine the motivation to learn and attend training and development courses.

General employee resistance to using know-how and further learning

The main reasons why employees do not make the maximum use of their know-how and creativity, and show a resistance to further learning and training, stem from the anti-learning pressures of the traditional hierarchical culture. They include:

- The block to employee involvement in decision-making. Views, ideas and suggestions are not generally sought or listened to by hierarchical supervisors and managers.
- A climate of cost-cutting, distrust and judgemental intolerance, creating:
  - fear of suggesting something different or opposing existing ideas and practices;
  - fear of giving feedback, especially to supervisors and other managers;
  - fear of admitting lack of understanding;
  - fear of saying they have a problem and requesting help;
  - fear of making a mistake;
  - pressure of high workloads and long working hours (heightened by downsizing);
  - cost-driven targets;
  - low or perceived unfair pay;
  - fear of job loss, adding to employees' disaffection and cynicism which undermines:
    (a) quality and customer care programmes (see also Chapter 4)

(b) motivation to learn and attend training and development courses.

In a collaborative culture where top management respects and values people and their contribution, gives them space to reflect, to learn, and to express their creativity, and gives them fair treatment relating to pay and job security, people are motivated to continuously learn and do a good job. In contrast, in a hierarchical culture where top management has a lack of respect for and trust in people and their contribution, blocks creativity and learning through judgemental, power-based, cost-focused relationships and structures, and treats them unjustly and unfairly in terms of pay and job security, people are demotivated from learning and doing their best.

It is unrealistic to expect people to be committed to 'working their socks off' trying to gain more knowledge and skills to improve their efficiency and come up with ideas and suggestions to benefit an organization, when, for example, there are perceived to be unfair job cuts and there is a general sense of insecurity; when they are subjected to pay restraints when top salaries are increased; and above all, when they are not empowered in their work. Significantly, there has been a growth in inequality in wages and earnings to a greater extent in Britain than in almost all other developed economies. This has been matched by a widening in the inequalities of influence and access to key decisions about work and employment (Millward, 1994, p. 133).

Examples: conflicting messages, job security, and performance

ILFORD In Chapter 3, ILFORD[2] was cited as an example where top management are developing and deploying more open, less arrogant, people-centred attitudes and skills, and a re-enforcing structure with reduced layers in the hierarchy, a system of departmental and cross-departmental teams, and a more horizontal pay system, etc. However, remnants of traditional hierarchical attitudes at the top were revealed in a programme of redundancies, which inevitably will have created insecurity and lack of trust, re-kindling and re-enforcing negative anti-learning attitudes, and therefore working against the definite gains they had achieved. In line with this, a reluctance towards the changes required for their TQM programme has been identified among some employees. Some of the union full-time officials and craft stewards, and sections of the supervisors have been reported to be anxious about the implications of TQM. Following the round of redundancies, employees expressed their doubts about the programme with the claim that: 'the first person to be made redundant last year was Deming!'

IPM Report   A survey by the Institute of Personnel Management (IPM)[3] reported that a majority of managers and supervisors expressed concerns about adapting to or accepting QM. Many merely paid lip-service to the quality process, while complaining and articulating anxieties about:

- loss of authority
- new programmes and targets which impose even higher workloads on an already stretched resource
- a clash between their conception of a quality service and what was expected of them under QM
- lack of job security.

Similar concerns were expressed by non-managerial employees. The situation has led to lowered employee commitment to introducing new ideas connected with the quality initiative.

Milliken Industrials   This American textile group realized early on in their application of a Total Quality approach, that employees would be de-motivated from improving their efficiency and fear that they might be eliminating their own or someone else's job, unless given an assurance that people would not be fired as a result of efficiency/quality improvements but instead be redeployed, retrained and reassigned. The managing director of the European branch comments[4]:

We believe it is appropriate to provide that sort of trust and security if we want people to give us their trust and to give us their contributions.

Nissan   When an ambitious expansion programme by Nissan UK[5] was affected by the downturn in Europe, they did not seek to scale down through a redundancy programme. Instead, the nightshift was suspended and Nissan's 2400 production staff put on to alternate weeks on day shift for 4 months. They endeavoured to provide numerous alternatives for employees. When it was recognized in late 1993 that the problem was likely to continue, the company suggested that it could be handled either by reducing headcount and having those who remained going back to full-time working, or by keeping everyone on and continuing with short-time working. It was the workers' choice to go for the former. No pressure was put on them by management, there was no target for job reduction, and the subsequent programme was called 'Separation by Agreement'. Uptake was mainly from people who had plans to work elsewhere or go back to college. Request for the package by some workers was not agreed to by management where the employee's skills were seen as indispensable.

Moreover, this choice given to employees was against a background where they knew that money was not being disproportionately and unfairly directed towards share dividends, top and middle management salaries and bonuses, and management perks. The situation, therefore, was significantly different from the usual 'head-count' approach to redundancy, even voluntary redundancy, within the traditional hierarchical Western organization. Nissan took this approach because, as it was pointed out at the time by personnel director, Peter Wickens, they have 'an absolute commitment to security of employment'. The reason for this is a recognition, not present in traditional Western companies, that this security and fair treatment of the workforce is essential for delivering the continuous learning needed for high quality, efficiency and innovation.

Nissan suppliers

To capitalize on extra employee time available due to the production downturn, many Nissan suppliers[6] have prevented redundancies by bringing forward training programmes, stepping up brainstorming on quality, and undergoing exhaustive analysis of their line layouts and production methods. They have opted to bring all their workforce into work each day by deploying those not needed for production on improvements to organization, quality, costs and delivery. The culture behind these moves is well summed up by an industrial reporter:

Redundancies [are not] an easy option for suppliers imbued with the culture of continuous improvement—or Kaizen as the Japanese call it. Their carefully selected workforces have been encouraged to unstinting effort by the expectation of secure employment.

Moreover, sacrificing expensively trained, high quality employees could prove shortsighted if, as the motor trade hopes, the European market picks up before too long.

It is this ability to go beyond the rhetoric prevalent in Western companies, and genuinely to give the highest respect and value to the human resource and their skills, which is the key to the successful long-term approach and superior performance of the Japanese.

The privatized utilities

Job loss has been a feature of all the privatized utilities[7]. At the same time there have been complaints of high prices, high profits, high share dividends, high share prices, high severance payments, and what have been referred to as excessive salaries and financial packages (bonuses, share options, pensions) for board members. The situation has led to the widespread attack that employees and customers are being treated unfairly.

The situation undermines employee learning and performance, as exemplified by the response to one announcement of further redundancies in British Gas's programme of job cuts. Both worker and union responses were negative, despite reassurance that there would be no compulsory redundancies. Union leaders expressed distrust and cynicism in the reassurance, fuelled by the fact that the company continued to increase dividends to shareholders. The response of some of the workers, broadcast in the media immediately after the announcement, indicated a similar distrust, and its negative effect on morale and motivation:

All our hard work's gone down the pan at the moment. So a matter of months now, 8 months or so, then it's redundancy I imagine. There's not much future.

The mood has been bad for a while. We knew that our jobs were on the line. To be quite honest we're all just waiting for our redundancy notices.

This is *not* an environment conducive to motivation, learning and improvement needed for high performance and added value, despite abundant rhetoric on customer care. As the company continued in its programme of cutting staff, restraining staff pay increases, and closing showrooms, employee concern grew and customer care increasingly was undermined (e.g. complaints were up by 172 per cent on the year in January 1995 according to the Gas Consumer Council). Not only will reduced numbers of employees have undermined the service, but, according to the Gas Consumer Council, it will also have been partly attributable to British Gas employees being uncertain about their jobs, causing them not to do their work as well as they should. The reported 75 per cent increase in the chief executive's pay and high levels of pre-tax profit against this background caused uproar across the political spectrum. The company claimed that the cost-cutting measures were necessary to meet the challenge of imminent competition (compare with Japanese example, Chapter 7).

Increased efficiency and performance is undoubtedly needed in the climate of keen competitors at home and the need to expand into overseas markets, and may be this would ultimately require some human resource 'leaning'. However, the example shows that to centre competitiveness on cost-cutting, and to centre cost-cutting on labour costs (see Chapter 1) without first involving the workforce (who are often best placed to come up with ideas for improving efficiency) and while unfairly increasing income for top managers and shareholders, only brings short-term 'bottom-line' gains, while undermining employee performance and customer satisfaction needed to maintain market share against growing competition.

Rover Cars   When Rover Cars[8] began to introduce Japanese working practices in the late 1980s, it included among other things an emphasis on teamworking where people would be constantly looking for better ways of doing things. This 'continuous improvement' approach was incompatible with the traditional ways of working, as one shift manager recollects:

In the old days, [people] knew that if they came forward with an efficiency improvement that somebody somewhere would lose their job.

Management realized, therefore, that for the new practices to succeed, there would need to be a change in contractual obligations and structure, including a 'jobs-for-life' pledge of no more forced redundancies:

> We recognized that you could only encourage anyone to create this level of change, radical change, of different ways of working, if at the same time they believe that they have a sense of security in that process, and they don't believe that they're working to actually rid themselves of a job. (*Managing director*)

> Now they are willing to come forward with the efficiency improvements knowing that we're going to look after the person who would lose his job. He will be found a job elsewhere within the plant. He has now got a job for life. (*Shift manager*)

(See also example at the end of this chapter.)

The job security-learning link: a summary

The link between job security and motivation, learning and innovation, is activated in two main ways in the traditional hierarchical company:

1 The widespread practice of cost-cutting through job loss: creating job insecurity which undermines people's motivation and ability to learn, train, and innovate.
2 The practice of making someone redundant when they learn and make innovative efficiency improvements: creating a fear of job loss undermining potential learning and improvements.

Contrast   In the traditional hierarchical culture, learning and improvements decrease job security. In a collaborative team culture, learning and improvements increase job security (Figure 6.1).

In a hierarchical culture, therefore, those responsible for training and people development generally, are not likely to have allies among the employees, and they should not waste all their time, as so often happens, trying to 'win over' employees to the merits of training and development. Most employees in fact know full well the merits of knowledge and skills, and would jump at the opportunity to fully use and improve them for the benefit of their organization, in the right environment. Any antagonism they show will result from disillusionment with the culture. It follows that a training/HR manager's time will be more effectively spent if, in the first instance, he or she directs their energies to persuading, involving and developing top management's core attitudes and skills as the basis for creating a secure learning and training environment (see below).

Traditional hierarchical culture

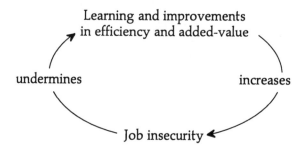

Collaborative team culture

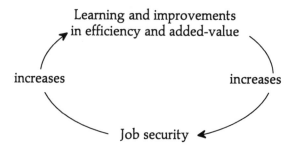

Figure 6.1 *The job security—learning link*

Traditional
learning–
training pitfalls

- The use of a great deal of rhetoric about the importance of people empowerment, skills and training, in place of action—by those in management.
- The tendency to create a facade by, for example:
  - applying the rhetoric of teamwork, employee involvement, empowerment, etc. to describe hierarchically run groups where employees' views are not sought or acted upon;
  - using the rhetoric of teamwork and human resource value, while applying 'mindless' cost-cutting through job cuts;
  - substituting 'communication' for 'employee involvement', in the form of top-down information bulletins, newsletters, etc.

  These reduce employee morale and create distrust and cynicism, leading to reduced learning and performance.
- The inability to understand the root and branch attitudinal changes needed from the top to convert the rhetoric into effective action.
- The tendency of hierarchical top managers to hand over responsibility for performance improvements to others, and to hide behind schemes, systems and techniques such as, e.g.:
  - quality control departments
  - quality control circles
  - external consultants

- BS 5750
- performance-related pay
- investors in people
- mission or policy statements
- codes of ethics
- suggestion schemes
- benchmarking
- Kaizen

As considered above, systems and schemes will not be effective, nor the people development and training they involve, if used as add-ons to the traditional culture. They specifically need to incorporate the development of a collaborative team culture involving core skills development from the top (see Chapter 12). Furthermore, the use of quality control departments works against the development of a *genuine* team culture by removing responsibility for quality and other outcomes from employees. Similarly, so can the use of external consultants, which can disenable employees, who know most about a job, from becoming the architects of change and improvement. Individual performance pay such as performance-related pay, is divisive, prone to unfairness, and often used to increase management control. It therefore works against genuine team building and learning. And quality systems such as BS 5750 tend to lock people into bureaucratic and rigid procedures, blocking change, creativity, innovation, learning, and continuous improvement.

Unless the culture issue is addressed, therefore, any particular strategy, and any particular task-orientated skill development programme, will not be fully cost-effective, and at worst will be wasteful and counterproductive. Deep-seated attitudes need to be changed from the tops of organizations for the widespread rhetoric on teamwork, employee empowerment and development, and customer care, to be translated into effective practice. For success, therefore, a broad learning strategy needs to be devised which incorporates culture and core skills development from the top.

Priority aims for training and HR managers

Those with overall responsibility for employee development and training should focus on:

- The need for the top manager to be aware of the key importance of culture to effective development and training.
- The need for the top manager to be *actively* committed to culture change.
- The need to work with human resource/personnel managers to:
  - persuade and gain the commitment of the top manager to developing a horizontal team structure (see next section);
  - devise and implement a collaborative team training and development programme from the top down (see Chapter 12).

Structural manifestations of a learning culture

Structural manifestations of top management attitudes and skills

A top manager with collaborative attitudes and skills will create an organizational structure which re-enforces reciprocal relationships and facilitates dialogue and learning. In contrast, a top manager with embedded hierarchical attitudes and behaviours will create a diametrically opposed organizational structure which re-enforces power-based relationships and one-way monologue, blocking dialogue and learning.

In reality, most organizations fall somewhere in between these two extremes, ranging *from*:

- those with top managers who mainly pay lip-service to employee involvement and development, and deploy quality programmes and HR involvement techniques purely as add-ons;

to:

- those with top managers who have gone some way to developing and breeding collaborative attitudes and skills, and the team structure that re-enforces them.

Within this range, all organizations are prey to performance impairment as a result of employees' reaction to contradictory messages from the top, as was considered above. The conflict will be most stark in the former situation. However, in the latter situation, where an organization has had definite success in deploying a more collaborative approach with employees, a conflicting message from the top can create as great a cynicism and resentment, and perhaps an even greater sense of hoax and betrayal of trust in employees, as was cited earlier in this chapter for the ILFORD case.

The collaborative organizational structure

The following moves to a more horizontal or flatter organizational structure are a sign of collaborative attitudes and skills in a top manager and his or her genuine commitment to developing a team culture. Only when a top manager is able truly to devolve responsibility to all employees and create equal-footing interactions between team leader and team member, manager and employee, will he or she be able to make these moves. As indicated, each move is linked with unleashing learning and skill development.

Top management commitment checklist

Remove:

- *Management layers to leave fewer levels of the hierarchy* which greatly slow communication and separate those taking decisions from those who know about the job, which stifles involvement and learning.

- *Quality departments and inspectors,*
  which are ineffective and stifle employee involvement and learning.
- *Training departments*
  which tend to remove responsibility for training from team leader and team member, stifling involvement and learning.
- *Judgemental management appraisal and evaluation systems*
  which are ineffective and stifle involvement, openness and learning.
- *Individual reward and promotion systems for managers based on short-term output and numerical performance measures*
  which are often unfair, oppressive, ineffective, and divisive, and therefore stifle teamwork and learning.
- *Individual reward systems (e.g. piece work; performance-related pay – which can reward favourites irrespective of true merit)*
  which are oppressive and divisive and stifle teamwork and learning.
- *Reward and promotion systems which ignore ideas, team-learning skills and ability to develop others, and are based more on favouritism, status, position, ladder-climbing and promotion politics (looking good in the eyes of the boss, etc.)*
  which are divisive and stifle teamwork and learning.
- *Inflexible distinctions between white and blue collar, manual and non-manual workers*
  which are divisive and work against teamwork and therefore learning.
- *Inflexible written job descriptions and demarcations between jobs, with correspondingly different pay systems*
  which are divisive, block interchanging teams and cross-fertilization of ideas, and therefore stifle multiskilling and learning generally.
- *Clocking on and salary deductions for lateness or absenteeism*
  which stifles motivation and learning.

Introduce:

- *Single status facilities and conditions of employment*:
  - the same overalls for every manager and employee
  - the same canteen
  - the same car parking (no reserved parking)
  - the same lockers or showers (no reserved lockers or showers)
  - the same method of pay
  - the same pension
  - the same sick pay
  - the same holidays
  which facilitate employee involvement and commitment to learning and improvement.
- *A job security pledge of no more forced redundancies*
  which creates employee commitment to learning and maximum effort.

- *A streamlined trade union agreement, with one voice representing all*
  which facilitates manager–employee communication, consultation, involvement and learning.
- *A channel of direct two-way communication between the top manager and the workforce*
  enabling open critical feedback and ideas from employees, which facilitates involvement and learning.
- *A system where all employees work in informal (ideally self-managed) teams, with responsibility for decisions on how to divide up tasks, projects, quality and other outcomes*
  which facilitates involvement, teamwork, multiskilling and general learning.
- *A flexible system of interchanging people between teams in different functions*
  which facilitates involvement, multiskilling and general learning.
- *Practical support and recognition for team-learning skills, ideas and collaborative involvement; and, if managers, for developing and enabling team members*
  which enhances learning and teamwork.
- *Sole reliance on continuous self-team appraisal and evaluation*
  which enhances teamwork and learning.
- *Team (non-financial) reward in the form of recognition and practical support*
  which enhance teamwork and learning.

All those people in an organization who are responsible for employee development, therefore, should:

Be aware of

- The influence of what are usually perceived as separate and irrelevant structural issues on the effectiveness of learning, training and performance.
- The constant undermining and waste of trainers' and trainees' time, effort and money in the traditional hierarchical organizational culture and structure.
- The consequent priorities for training and HR managers (previous section).

The above checklist is modelled on the collaborative structure in successful Japanese companies, and top managers with the core collaborative attitudes and skills will find no difficulty implementing these moves. Typically, Western organizations comply to the list in varying degrees.

Example   The importance of organizational structure to bringing about a learning culture is illustrated in the case of the Rover Group.[9] According to the Group's personnel director, 'Rover has embraced a style of management that has replaced the traditional hierarchical functional organization through an emphasis on process and culture.' Changes in culture and structure were initiated by superior Japanese competition and the influence of Rover's partner Honda. In 1986, Rover managers visited the Honda plant in Marysville, Ohio, and were inspired to organize an attitude survey of their own workers. This revealed that systems, processes, procedures, and management style and priorities, were all hindrances to achieving high quality of performance.

Workers indicated that they were not being allowed to do the quality job they wished. Most employees did not feel that the best use was being made of their talents and that they:

- were not being given sufficient challenge
- were not involved in problem-solving
- did not enjoy a relationship of mutual trust with their boss
- did not have clear opportunities to develop themselves
- did not receive recognition for contribution or achievement.

Moves were made to change the organizational structure to meet these concerns. Eleven layers of manufacturing organization were reduced to 6. The traditional autocratic role of production foremen was changed to non-disciplinary team leader. Teams were given responsibility for production, housekeeping, continuous improvement of process and product, quality control and inventories.

Corporate and employee development was facilitated through an in-house Learning Centre. Further vehicles of involvement were developed besides teamworking, such as a suggestion scheme, discussion groups and workshops. Also, voluntary groups have been established to review management practice, concentrating on culture, style and behaviour, putting development routes in place for leaders and managers.

These moves to a more open, learning culture required a change in the traditional terms and conditions of employment which were no longer appropriate. Wholesale change in contractual obligations with employees was necessary, and these came into operation in April 1992. They included:

- no clocking on
- single status terms
- the removal of separate hourly paid and staff grade structures
- security of employment.

The latter condition is seen as paramount. A major concern expressed, for example, by the personnel director after the Group's acquisition by BMW, was that this key condition should be adhered to by the new owners, as it would be 'against BMW's best interests to start getting rid of a committed and involved workforce'.

Exercise: a strategy for training and HR managers

1 Use the above checklist to gauge how far in reality your organization has moved towards a genuine team culture.

2 If your organization has made no, or a very limited number of, moves, begin to work together (training, human resource/personnel managers) to compile a succinct presentation to persuade the top manager of the need for culture change. This could include the following:

(a) *The results of a workforce attitude survey*
Gain top management agreement to undertake an attitude survey of employees to find out what they think of the organization. Questions should cover areas such as:
(i)   Do you think the best use is being made of your talents?
(ii) Are you being given challenging and satisfying work?
(iii) Are you involved in problem-solving and decision-making?
(iv) Do you enjoy a relationship of mutual trust with your boss?
(v)   Are you provided with clear opportunities to develop yourself, e.g. through training or job rotation?
(vi) Are you given recognition and support for contribution or achievement?

(b) *An indication of examples of best practice*
Examples of organizations which have greatly improved performance and competitiveness through starting to develop a collaborative team approach with employees, suppliers and customers.

(c) *A list of benefits*[10]
(i)   Creation of a highly committed and motivated workforce.
(ii)   A workforce which can fully utilize its knowledge and skills to maximize efficiency, quality and innovation.
(iii) The full and effective use of existing equipment.
(iv)   Continuous, cost-free learning and skill development.
(v)   Avoidance of wasteful training.
(vi)   Avoidance of costly 'add-on' stress management schemes and techniques such as counselling, on-site massage, etc., which have a limited effect.
(vii) Avoidance of high financial penalties by increasingly critical and selective insurance companies regarding systems for dealing with stress.
(viii) Reduced price insurance policies.
(ix)   Avoidance of being sued by employees for stress.
(x)   Excellent industrial relations.

(d) *An indication of the culture change strategy required*
This would be centred on:
(i)   An integrated work-based team training and development programme starting with the top manager (see Chapters 11 and 12).
(ii) Structural goals (as above checklist).

Those Western organizations that have gone some way towards developing a collaborative team culture and structure, will also benefit further by implementing a training and development programme to build an integrated work-based team-learning approach as prescribed in Chapters 11 and 12.

Notes

1. See, for example, RSA (1994) as in references for Chapter 2.
2. Based on case study in *Quality: People Management Matters*, 1993, Institute of Personnel Management (subsequently Institute of Personnel and Development). Any interpretations are this author's.
3. Reported in Note 2.
4. Quotation and information from *In Business*, BBC Radio 4, 31 March 1993.
5. Based on private communication with Peter Wickens, former personnel director Nissan UK, 1995.
6. Quotation and information from, 'How Nissan suppliers are using training to fight hard times', by Chris Tinghe, *Financial Times*, 21 December 1993.
7. Quotations from media reports.
8. Quotations transcribed from: *Business Matters*, BBC 2, 29 July 1993; *High Interest*, Channel Four, 23 January 1994.
9. Based on: 'Unleashing the Potential of People', by D.G. Bower, personnel director of the Rover Group, in *Industrial and Commercial Training*, Vol.26, No.2, 1994.
10. Chapter 7 indicates further benefits.

Reference

Millward N. (1994). *The New Industrial Relations?* (Policy Studies Institute, London).

7 Traditional blocks on survivability: the costs of not changing to a learning culture

Earlier chapters have considered how the traditional and still prevailing hierarchical organization blocks learning skills development from the top, and thereby undermines a company's potential to maximize efficiency and added-value necessary for competitiveness and survival. This chapter will consider further the costs of not changing to a learning culture providing additional support for trainers and ammunition for training and human resource managers.

Hierarchical organizations lose out in a number of areas, some of which have already been touched on. The key areas are as follows:

- Loss of on-going learning and added-value.
- Loss of cost-effective training.
- Loss of added-value through R&D.

Loss of on-going learning and added-value

Key front-line staff Still little realized by those in top positions in organizations, the only people who can deliver and guarantee efficiency and quality in processes, product and service, are those who are actually doing the job, i.e. the front-line workforce. It should be obvious, but is not, that they are the ones best placed to come up with ideas for making improvements and innovations in the three key areas: not managers who are often remote from the job and the customer.

This realization is a key factor which distinguishes high performance

Japanese companies from most of their Western counterparts. Managers in Japanese transplants in Britain will often point out how it is the minds of their employees, their creativity, which is the critical factor enabling them to increase productivity. And the following comment by a Japanese industrialist expresses just how misguided Western companies are:

We are going to win and the industrial West is going to lose out ... With your bosses doing the thinking while the workers wield the screwdrivers, you are convinced deep down that this is the right way to run a business. For you the essence of management is getting the ideas out of the heads of the bosses and into the hands of labour. The survival of firms today is so hazardous in an increasingly unpredictable environment that their continued existence depends on the day-to-day mobilization of every ounce of intelligence. For us the core of management is the art of mobilizing and putting together the intellectual resources of all employees in the service of the firm.[1]

Barriers to intelligence   In the traditional hierarchical organization, employees strongly feel the barriers preventing them from fully applying their knowledge and skills (considered in Chapter 6), and from delivering the levels of efficiency, quality and innovation which they know they can achieve. They typically feel underused and devalued. The feeling of being undervalued and merely being a statistic that can be disposed of in the future, has been heightened with the increase of company downsizing, and the use of fixed-term and part-time contracts.

Front-line blocking   This 'exclusive' culture creates a reaction in employees. They become demotivated from applying and further developing their knowledge and skills. In addition to this, they will also often expend time and energy working against their supervisors or managers in certain ways, further undermining efficiency, quality and innovation. For example, people typically withhold information even though they are aware it will prevent a mishap or make an improvement. They will shun any training and development courses their organization introduces or recommends. In short, there will be a lack of good will, loyalty and commitment. (This also increasingly applies to middle management as downsizing affects them.) The traditional individualistic approach of top managers, governed by short-term self-interest, is being matched by a corresponding antagonistic individualistic self-interest approach in front-line staff and middle managers. There is also a knock-on anti-learning approach with suppliers and customers, referred to in Chapter 4.

The cost of this (and the factors considered below) to learning and added-value is reflected in an analysis of business activity undertaken by the Toyota production system. This showed that:[2]

- 65 per cent is wasted (non value-added)
- 30 per cent is necessary but not value-added
- 5 per cent is value-added.

Within the supply chain added-value remains at 5 per cent while costs go up, with everyone 'grabbing what they can for themselves in the short term'.

Example   For decades, the motor giant General Motors operated a hierarchical bureaucratic culture where most things were directly controlled by top management.[3] Retired workers recall how their bosses squandered money on poor investments. In one case they were put to work 7 days a week setting up a new production line which was to produce exhaust manifolds. It was never used. In another example an electronic train was made to transport parts and eliminate fork-lift drivers. Millions of dollars were spent on it, and it was used for about 6 months and then scrapped. Another criticism against management was that it was out of touch with the car buying public, and it unilaterally sanctioned designs which turned out to be 'turkeys'—contributing to General Motors' loss of market share. If employees down the line had had input before such decisions were made, then the decline in market share and runaway costs which plunged the corporation into crisis by the 1990s, threatening its very existence, would have been avoided.

Contrast   Collaborative working cultures give responsibility and long-term involvement to employees, and encourage and facilitate the continuous development and use of team-learning skills of the kinds considered in previous chapters. This:

- Unleashes full skill potential and creativity.
- Makes employees eager to:
  - fully apply their knowledge and skills to avoid rejects and eliminate waste;
  - point out defects in the product or process;
  - give suggestions for improvement;
  - discuss problems and ideas outside work hours and take them home to think about.

Not only, therefore, is there on-going informal learning and training as people interact collaboratively in and between teams on the shop-floor and in team meetings. There is also a kind of continuous informal research and development. In contrast to the hierarchical approach, this continuous improvement leads to a steady reduction in wasted activity (e.g. there are numerous examples of large savings made by companies which genuinely involve the workforce), and a steady growth in added-value without overall costs increasing. The traditional command-and-control culture, by giving little to no responsibility and involvement to employees, loses this mainspring of continuous improvement in efficiency and added-value, thereby greatly undermining a company's chances of surviving.

Loss of cost-effective training

Traditional characteristics

Traditionally training has tended to be inadequate whether it has been on-the-job or course-based. The main characteristics have been:

1 Minimum to no on-the-job training.
2 Irrelevant training courses. This has disproportionally been directed to managerial levels rather than front-line employees, and there has been little effort to link it with the job and deploy learning after a course.

This situation has blocked cost-effective training, and in many cases has led to outright waste.

Characteristic 2 above is mostly restricted to large to medium-sized organizations, for the simple reason that small firms have relied mainly on on-the-job training (if any) in order that certain machines can be operated. Surveys undertaken in the first half of the 1990s showed that most small organizations remained reluctant to move beyond characteristic 1.

External constraints

It was considered in Chapter 2 that there are a number of external constraints on organizations which work against their investing time and money on skill development. One in particular, namely the treatment by banks, has been a greater constraint on small businesses than large. Banks have been condemned from a number of quarters for overstating risk and levelling higher margins and charges on small businesses than is warranted, and this has re-enforced the traditional quantitative difference in training between small and large organizations. The greater constraint on larger organizations has been shareholder pressure. Both of these constraints are mitigated by developing a learning culture.

Contrast

Collaborative learning cultures avoid 1 and 2 above. As considered in the previous section, on-going collaborative interaction in and between teams on the shop-floor means there will be continuous learning and informal training for all employees, through continuous interchange of information and mutual support. The benefit of developing a learning culture is at least two-fold for the small business:

- It will gain continuous, effective, cost-free on-the-job learning and training.
- The learning-team skills of communication, openness, etc., considered in the previous chapters, will enable the manager to effectively communicate with and keep informed their bank, creating a climate of trust as a basis for getting a fairer deal.[4]

A parallel benefit to the second benefit above is gained for larger organizations in relation to shareholders. Top managers in hierarchical organizations have tended:

- to try to cover problems up
- not to be straight
- to ignore shareholder interests at certain times
- not to take the opportunity to respond to shareholder concerns at appropriate times.

As institutional shareholders, following America's lead, increasingly move to become involved as owners vying to improve company performance, this behaviour at board level will no longer be tolerated, and risks lowered share price and ultimately hostile takeover.

Collaborative team-learning skills of openness, etc., in top managers (CEOs, chairpersons), will enable them to avoid the traditional secretive confrontational approach with shareholders (and non-executive directors) and instead:

- keep them well informed
- maintain a dialogue with them
- take open criticism and comment from them
- develop a constructive learning partnership with them

for the benefit of all a company's stakeholders.

Relevant training   In the case of organizations which develop a learning culture and which undertake formal training, the realization of the importance of the knowledge and skills of front-line workers, the close collaboration between employee and line manager, and the devolvement of decisions about training courses to those closest to the job, helps to ensure that training courses are relevant and knowledge and skills learned are deployed back in the workplace. This, in turn, helps to ensure that training is cost-effective. ILFORD, for example, have moved in this direction. The individual and the line manager:[5]

- discuss where the employee's job is going, if technology or any other issue is likely to change it, how it is likely to change it, etc.
- consider whether the employee has latent skills
- explore what additional skills and knowledge will be needed
- jointly agree on what training is needed
- predict what kind of difference it is likely to make
- consider the means by which to measure whether that difference is achieved after training.

At Motorola, in-house courses in management, engineering, manufacturing and sales, which typically run for 2 or 3 days, are closely tied to the workplace. For example, the performance of participants is not graded, but success is measured by change initiatives taken when they return to their job. At Unipart University there are no exams or degrees, no pass or fail, just an expectation of continuous learning to be applied in the workplace for the ultimate benefit of the customer (see also example in Chapter 8).

The above escape routes from the no-training and waste-training traps to cost-effective training, are therefore lost to companies which do not develop a collaborative learning culture. This greatly undermines efficiency and the capability for quality and innovation necessary for survival.

Training evaluation and cost-effective training

Cost-effective training is that which leads to the greatest improvement in individual performance, and through that, organizational performance, for the investment put in. A prevalent view, therefore, has been that in order to justify training expenditure, its effect on organizational performance needs to be evaluated. However, spending time and resources undertaking numerical measure of performance outcomes, e.g. the amount by which sales have increased, is of little value and wasteful because generally such an approach is:

- Too short-termist   There is a tendency to look for an immediate quantitative payback.
- Too simplistic   It neglects the many cultural factors/barriers of the kind already considered which affect skill deployment and performance in the workplace.
- Too historical   Evaluating an outcome gives no indication of how training should be changed if the outcome is poor.
- Too late   The evaluation measure occurs after the training has taken place, and the money already spent.

As this book has already considered, and will further indicate in subsequent chapters, the only way to *ensure* fully cost-effective training is through developing a genuine collaborative team culture. The futility of numerical measures of training outcomes (whether organizational or individual) is reflected in the training evaluation policy of some of those organizations which have begun the process of culture change, e.g. Motorola and Unipart mentioned in the previous sub-section.

Loss of added-value through R&D

Traditional hierarchical organizations have not given sufficient weight to research and development (see also next section). An extreme example of this is the notoriously hierarchical British construction industry. Characterized by adversarial management, delays, poor quality (defects cost up to £1000 million a year), and disputes, some people estimate that construction in Britain costs 30 per cent more than it should. According to a 1994 report headed by Sir Michael Latham, it is widely believed that the highly confrontational nature of the industry has meant that more money is channelled into litigation than into R&D, problem-solving, and developing expertise and new ideas. The outcome has been an industry which is at the bottom of the European construction league table, and a generally poor service which is in danger of being taken over by foreign competitors unless the culture is changed.

Also, any investment made in R&D in hierarchical companies, and even those that have begun to make changes in working culture, is unlikely to be cost-effective, as it is likely to be controlled by top managers out of touch with employees and customers.

Examples   Despite investment in R&D, prior to 1993 many of the areas the Lucas Group spent its money on turned out to be poor investments. Although the company had introduced more flexible Japanese-style teamworking, concern over the direction and level of investment (which was below that of its rivals), put a question on the quality of its management, and suggested that a team culture had not been fully developed.

Although there were great improvements in quality and customer service at Xerox by the late 1980s (considered in Chapters 3 and 4), the 're-inventing' of its industry necessary for long-term survival had been limited. High investment in R&D led to many innovatory ideas being proposed and developed by research employees during the 1980s (the mouse, personal computer, laser printer, and lap-top computer, etc.). However, top management failed to exploit these ideas. Instead they were left to other companies to convert into highly revolutionary and successful products. The events indicate that although there had been a move to increase employee involvement and empowerment through developing a team approach, it had been limited. The leadership still had some way to go before it reached the levels of humility, respect, ability to listen, etc., necessary to learn from and cost-effectively harness employees' ideas, and fully respond to and keep ahead of customer expectations vital for long-term survival (see also Chapter 11).

Contrast   High spending on R&D by successful Japanese organizations is made cost-effective through collaborative partnerships between managers, employees, suppliers and customers. There is a continuous interchange of ideas between all the players, and a continuous seeking out by management of employee, supplier and customer feedback. An aspect of this is the building of prototypes and field trials, i.e. testing out the product on real users. This involvement of and listening to the main players has been a cornerstone of successful Japanese companies' ability to anticipate, innovate, and exceed customer expectations.

Certain western companies also illustrate the value of R&D for learning organizations. An operations manager at Hewlett-Packard, for example, pointed out how having an R&D component means that people are in charge of their own destiny, which provides a lot of motivation to the whole business:

> They know that they own this group of customers, they're anticipating their needs, they come up with creative ideas. You wouldn't believe how much motivation you get in the team both in marketing, R&D and manufacturing when you do that.[6]

By not developing a collaborative learning culture, therefore, companies undervalue (see also next section) and fail to maximize the benefits of R&D. Those that do invest in it without culture change are in danger of:

- embarking on irrelevant avenues, or ones that will not be exploited
- wasting enormous investments of time, brain power and money
- undermining R&D potential to satisfy and exceed customer needs necessary for long-term survival.

Short-term profit or long-term learning

Chapter 6 considered that an indication that a top manager had or was developing the core collaborative team-learning skills as a basis for developing a genuine team culture, was if he or she was able to implement a more horizontal structure. A further indication of genuine commitment to culture change is when there is a priority of directing funds towards training, R&D and equipment.

Collaborative learning organizations are exceptional. Usually the cry is that there is not enough money for investment in equipment, training and R&D. Admittedly during recession there is likely to be a squeeze on profits making things difficult, and it was considered in Chapter 2 that, certainly in the UK, there is a general lack of a supportive framework from Government and investors to encourage and facilitate such long-term investments. But why do some companies overcome these difficulties? It is a matter of priorities.

Traditional 'anti-learning' priorities

Top managers in traditional hierarchically run organizations tend to give priority to:

- short-term profit
- share price and dividends
- top salaries
- acquisitions and mergers
- administration
- office furnishing
- perks.

There is a comparative reticence to putting funds towards what is seen as 'costly' training, R&D and equipment, which undermine the above priorities. This is linked with a culture of:

- short-term relationships with employees, suppliers and customers
- disinterest in the needs of end consumers
- self-interest and short-term personal gain.

Result: low motivation, minimum to poor quality, minimum to poor efficiency, low innovation, low responsiveness to customers, undermining long-term growth in market share and profit particularly during recession, reducing further the likelihood of investment in training, R&D and equipment. It is a vicious circle.

The 'investors in people' priorities

In contrast, top managers in collaborative working cultures give priority of funding towards developing the operating business by investing in:

- training
- R&D
- equipment.

There is an avoidance of spending on unnecessaries and excessive personal gain. This is linked with a culture of:

- understanding of consumers' needs and providing reliable, quality products
- productive long-term relationships with employees, suppliers and customers
- group interest and commitment.

Result: high motivation, high quality, high efficiency, high innovation, high responsiveness to customers, promoting long-term organic growth, increased market share and profit even during recession, increasing the ability for further investment in training, R&D and equipment. It is a virtuous circle.

Priority example

Seabait, the pioneering and successful small business referred to in Chapter 4, is a clear example[7] of a company which survived hardships and came through strongly by having a priority of directing resources towards the operating business: employee training, equipment and R&D, at the expense of other non-developmental expenditure. No money was spent on unnecessary 'frivolities' such as smart office furnishings, perks, etc. After 10 years the business still operated from portakabins, there was one part-time secretary, no dividends had yet been paid on shares, and there were virtually no perks. Not surprisingly, the 'top salaries' were well below the national average.

Contrasting cultures

Low investment relative to major competitors has prevailed for over a century in the UK (and to a certain extent the US). OECD and Government figures showed that manufacturing investment in the UK was lower in 1992 than in 1979, while main industrial competitors such as Japan and Germany raced ahead substantially increasing their investment. To a lesser extent, France's investment also increased over that period as did the US's. OECD figures in the mid 1990s also indicated that the UK invested less per head of population than France and America, and substantially lower than Germany and Japan. And the 1995 World Competitiveness Report indicated that the UK ranked 28th out of 48 countries in terms of investing sufficiently in the training of their employees. Rankings (based on responses of chief executives and economic leaders) included:

UK	5.10
US	5.65
France	6.38
Germany	7.27
Japan	8.04

This survey result is in line with the UK's Tendency to invest less than its major competitors. Although UK investment was growing, it was reported in 1995 to be less than half the 10 per cent rate predicted earlier by the Government.

Example 1 The above priority differences and the consequent effect on competitiveness, are illustrated in a report comparing the British and Japanese Motorcycle industries in 1975.[8] Major factors cited in the decline of the British industry were:

- A focusing on short-term profitability[9] creating:
  - chronic underinvestment, with mostly old, general purpose, fairly labour intensive equipment (net fixed investment per employee in 1973 was less than £1300);
  - small R&D facilities;
  - a history of acquisitions;
  - withdrawal from the smaller bikes market when levels of profitability declined when faced with Japanese competition;
  - financially driven restructuring—factory closures and redundancy programmes creating industrial dispute—leading to failure to introduce new models when profitability in the superbikes segment declined when faced with Japanese competition.
- Failure to integrate design management into the production and marketing process.
- A weak relationship with suppliers making them reluctant to invest on behalf of their customers.

Major factors cited in the rise of the Japanese industry were:

- A focusing on market share often at the expense of short-term profitability, through a focusing on long-term investment[10] enabling:
  - introduction of advanced production technology (net fixed investment per employee in 1973 was £4928);
  - large R&D facilities;
  - a high rate of technological and organizational learning and innovation reducing costs in design and manufacture;

- higher productivity enabling higher levels and increases of pay for employees than in British factories, while bringing down the real costs and prices of their products in the market place;
- introduction of modern technology together with growth enabling an avoidance of labour redundancies and 'scrap and build' programmes;
- a continuously improving marketing service, establishing larger distributors offering a better service to dealers, and larger dealers offering better sales and repair services to retail customers.
- An integrated design, production and marketing function.
- A close relationship with suppliers ensuring parallel technological development

Note   The above report comments:

The cost advantage of the Japanese is securely based on this higher productivity. It does not arise from lower labour costs: Japanese labour costs have been exceeding those in the British factories for a number of years and have consistently risen more rapidly on trend. (p.xiv)

This puts the lie to a prevalent western belief that it was lower pay which gave Japanese companies their competitive advantage over the West (see also Chapter 1 regarding labour costs).

Example 2   The culture of self-interest and personal gain in the UK and US is reflected in the very high levels of executive pay not generally matched in higher performing German and Japanese companies. It is also reflected in the practice of tying the personal fortunes of boards of directors with the share price of a company through share option deals. The concern is that this creates a potential conflict of interest, and militates against objective commercial and long-term investment decisions aimed at employee and product/service development, which are likely to lower share price and dividends.

Another concern relates to the potentially damaging effect on learning and performance caused by high inequality in incomes, not present to the same extent in more economically successful Japan or in certain other Asian countries.

The Asian Tigers have the most equal income distribution as well as being the fastest growing economies in the world.

Summary of costs created by hierarchical anti-learning attitudes

The above example illustrates that a top management which oversees poor and weak 'non-collaborative' internal and external relationships goes hand in hand with high priority on short-term profit, acquisitions, low investment in skill development, R&D and equipment, resulting in long-term uncompetitiveness.

> To survive against global competition, there needs to be a culture switch from short-term financial priorities still endemic in Western organisations to more collaborative long-term learning and development priorities.

The Institute of Management's 1994 survey: *Management Development to the Millennium*, which set out the key areas of management development needed for the long-term survival of companies, included the following in its list of skills and competencies for the managers of 2001:

Task skills that create the added-value firms need, such as analysis, prioritizing and benchmarking, will be essential but they must be able to approach these tasks with strong interpersonal skills that influence, coach and counsel their colleagues.

Companies involved in the survey acknowledged the importance of managers having a higher degree of interpersonal skills, comprising an ability to listen and relate to people. This reflected the increasing awareness of the importance of interpersonal skills in achieving what the survey referred to as 'fluid, less hierarchical and less functionally-orientated business structures'. As considered in previous chapters, core collaborative attitudes and skills at top management level are the hub of culture change and high performance, and without addressing this issue all the exhortations to managers to change organizations will come to little. However, as mentioned in Chapter 6, traditional 'macho' hierarchical attitudes have marginalized, trivialized, and sometimes ridiculed the vital 'soft' interpersonal attitudes and skills needed. The deep-rootedness of traditional attitudes means that it is taking time for the key skills to be given the prominence necessary to change practice effectively.

Without the core collaborative team-learning attitudes and skills of humility, respect, listening, etc., at top management level, an organization will not be able to:

- effectively and continuously harness the skills and knowledge of all employees to create on-going learning and innovation
- effectively respond to the development needs and gains of employees necessary for cost-effective training
- effectively learn from and respond to employees', suppliers' and

customers' ideas necessary for cost-effective R&D
- effectively learn from and respond to best practice
- effectively learn from and respond to national and global changes and influences on the organization.

The ultimate cost to organizations is that they will not survive.

Notes

1. Quoted in RSA (1994) as in References for Chapter 2.
2. Taken from videotape of University Launch, Unipart Group Ltd, 1993.
3. The information in this example is from *The Money Programme*, BBC, 23 January 1994. The interpretations are this author's.
4. See for example *Small Businesses and Their Banks 1994*, Reports 1 and 2, by Martin Binks and Christine Ennew, Nottingham University, 1994, which consider the need for openness and better communication as the key to better relationships with, and treatment by, banks.
5. From an interview with the director of Human Resources, December 1993.
6. Comment in *In Business*, BBC Radio 4, 27 November 1994.
7. From private communication with managing director, Peter Cowin.
8. Information taken from *Strategy Alternatives for the British Motorcycle Industry*, a report prepared for the Secretary of State for Industry by the Boston Consulting Group Ltd. House of Commons paper 532, Vol. 14, HMSO, London, 1975.
9. This will have been reinforced by external factors such as short-term pressures of financial institutions, as referred to in Chapter 2.
10. This will have been reinforced by external factors, such as supportive long-term financial institutions.

8 Training approaches

This chapter will consider:

- The training methods increasingly preferred by organizations
- The influence of culture change and external training providers in that growing preference
- The need for culture change to be taken further to achieve fully cost-effective training

Work-related training

The perception by small businesses that external training is irrelevant, and the traditional tendency for larger organizations to countenance wasteful and costly irrelevant training, has been compounded by the fact that external training providers have traditionally offered irrelevant, theoretical academic courses. Increasing competition posed by the global market place and recession have led to organizational responses which include drives for quality, technological change and organizational restructuring. This has been the trigger for seeking:

- more training
- more cost-effective training

It is the need for cost-effective training which has caused the shift away from traditional external training over recent years. The biggest increases have been in the areas of:

- in-house courses and programmes
- on-the-job training
- coaching/mentoring
- flexible/open learning

Tailored training

In contrast to traditional external courses, such internal and open training approaches can be tailored to fit workplace needs and goals, making them more cost-effective. The cost-effectiveness has been increased further by the move in some organizations to devolve training decisions and delivery to line managers who are closest to employee and job needs (see ILFORD example in Chapter 7). Ideal characteristics include:

- Line managers as key enablers, facilitators and coaches.
- An internal network of trainers, providing:
  - training for line managers to enable them to fulfil their on-the-job training and coaching role;
  - internal specialists—other line managers, department heads, directors, etc.—who could be called on by line managers;
- An in-company learning centre providing general learning support to all employees.

This devolution of training decisions is linked with an increase in the general belief that many management decisions are more effective when taken down the line than when imposed top-down by specialists.

The flexible nature of distance- or open-learning courses such as those provided by the Open College and the Open University, can also enable a more tailored approach by allowing the trainee to use learning material at their own pace and in their own workplace, helped by open-learning tutors and workplace mentors. Increase in cost-effectiveness by moving away from less relevant external courses to tailored work-related training, has enabled organizations to have more training, and more effective training, while not increasing their training budgets.

Changing external training

Off-the-shelf shortcomings

As companies increasingly see work-related training to be of importance and in-house training the best way forward for achieving it, the traditional approach of external trainers needs to change.

Criticisms typically made against external training providers and consultants include:

- they are too expensive
- courses are inflexible and not relevant
  - contain unnecessary information/irrelevant examples
  - too theoretical
- courses offered at inflexible times
- they do not understand the firm's difficulties
- they do not understand the firms training needs
- they are disruptive
- they invent problems

These are shortcomings experienced by small and large companies alike. For example, the human resource director in a division of one large company voiced the following concerns to me:

Educational establishments still tend to have products which they have available for you, rather than say, 'What are your needs, and can we use our expertise to design and deliver something which will meet your organization, say supervisor training?'. We will go to ... and say, 'Well look, this is how we see our supervisors developing over the next five years, we think we should have some of this, some of that, and some of the other'. What they say is 'Well we have a ... course available', and then you have to almost twist arms to get certain parts of that course modified so that you can even use company case studies by way of examples, rather than some hypothetical ones which they have in their portfolio, but which will mean nothing to your employees. So I do have concerns around that interface.

The remote off-the-shelf traditional approach is not just a characteristic of educational establishments and private providers. Off-the-shelf Government initiatives, such as NVQs, have been criticized for their bureaucracy and irrelevance where there is excess paperwork, a mismatch between real business needs and the prescribed areas of competence in the qualifications, and too low a standard. The irrelevance of training for the unemployed has also been criticized, voiced here by Nottinghamshire TEC chief executive:

What the Government is doing generally in terms of programmes for unemployed people is keeping them apart from employers. ... you have a training programme for instance ... which is completely separate from and doesn't have impact on employers.

In these respects, therefore, the Government has been out of step with the move towards a tailored approach to training.

Industry–education partnerships   To remove the above concerns, external training providers will need to recognize and respond to the differing needs of users, and work in partnership with them to decide:

- course content
- course time
- course location.

External providers need to work with users to develop relevant courses where the theory is tied to relevant practical examples, at flexible times, and with trainers going out to the workplace as much as possible. In this the development of collaborative cultures is a key factor, as will be considered in the next section.

The human resource director referred to above recognized that there are times when they have to call on the expertise of external providers. In the increasingly competitive environment in which educational providers, private providers and consultants are operating, those that are unable to change their approach will lose custom to those that do.

Collaborative training

It has been considered that the move towards more practically relevant work-related training has been triggered by recession and increased competition, which necessitate a greater amount of training and more cost-effective training. There are in fact three main requirements for training to be fully cost-effective. It must be:

- work-related
- hands-on
- collaborative.

Work-related training

Traditional external courses have been too theoretical and used remote often unrealistic practical examples, if any. The human resource director referred to in the previous section indicates the importance of tailoring course content to the workplace, and the inadequacy of traditional training in this respect.

If [trainees] see somebody they work with or they know works within and understands the business, and if they are presenting the information and developing the skills using examples from the business, it's much more credible [than an external provider using examples from other businesses] and people relate to it more, and are motivated to buy into what's going on.

> Work-related training, tying theory to practical examples which directly relate to trainees' workplaces, enhances their motivation and understanding.

Hands-on training

Traditionally, not only have students and trainees had to sit through theory where there is little to no attempt to relate it directly to their work, but they have had to be totally passive recipients of information. The superficial role of the student in the traditional lecture approach has been:

- passive receptor of irrelevant theoretical information
- cramming for exams
- regurgitating data
- retain little knowledge
- difficulty in understanding knowledge and how to apply it, i.e. skill incompetence.

This represents what is referred to as 'surface learning' as opposed to 'deep learning'. The ineffectiveness of this approach is leading organizations to go for training which is both work-related, and which requires the active involvement of the trainee.

Hands-on approaches include the use of:

- projects based on the use of equipment and techniques in a realistic simulation or in the workplace

- project-related assignments.

A hands-on approach, which gives students the opportunity to apply the knowledge and practise the skill in as real a situation as possible, deepens their understanding of knowledge and how to apply it.

Examples
1 Increasingly business schools are working with companies to design, deliver and assess flexible management programmes, incorporating learning on the job with the involvement of company managers as mentors.
2 The University of Sunderland, in partnership with companies such as Nissan, have devised an automotive design and manufacture degree course which bases the students in a design studio which simulates as much as possible an engineering workplace environment. Within this environment students undertake projects and assignments in line with what would be expected of them in the workplace. The studio is designed to give each student a computer at his or her desk, equipped with packages used by working engineers as well as standard information technology packages. To support projects the course has specialist subjects such as design, manufacture, analysis, materials, electronics and management.

> Hands-on training leads to a better understanding of knowledge and how to apply it, than being a purely passive receptor of information

Knowing how and knowing why
There is the danger of the pendulum swinging too far in the direction of practical hands-on training. This criticism, for example, has been levied against the NVQ system (e.g. Smithers, 1993). The concerns of some vocational bodies and experts is that the qualifications concentrate on the ability of trainees to undertake narrowly specified practical tasks, and there is a lack of theory and basic principles necessary for knowledge, understanding and flexibility[1]. Therefore, someone might know *how* to carry out a particular task, but without knowing *why*—background theory and principles—they will:

- not have a deep understanding of the properties of the materials they are dealing with, and the nature and limits of the tools
- be unable to apply their skills with precision
- be unable to apply their skills to cope with unfamiliar situations
- be unable to extend their skills to cope with changes in technology.

Trainees would then be comparable with a computer which has been programmed just for one simple task. An underlying concern is the superiority of European vocational training. In Germany, France and Holland, for example, theoretical and academic learning are regarded as vital complements to vocational studies, and pupils are generally considered to be two or three years ahead of their British counterparts.

> Knowing how to do something effectively depends on knowing why

To achieve effective learning and training, therefore, theory must not be removed or watered down, but tied closely to work-related practical examples and the hands-on experience of trainees.

Collaborative training

Work-related, hands-on training is more effective, and therefore, more cost-effective, than the traditional academic theoretical approach. There is a third factor, however, needed to make training fully cost-effective.

Authoritarian blocking

Even when training is work-related and hands-on, it can still be, and often is, undertaken didactically. The trainer/manager operates in an authoritarian manner, and goes beyond the mere communication of factual information to the:

- imposition of theory and 'knowledge' as a closed, unchallengeable fact reflected in a static, fixed curriculum
- imposition of opinions
- imposition of decisions (e.g. on essays, projects, assignments)
- imposition of top-down, one-way assessment.

Students might be involved in practical activity, but they are still passive receptors of information. The trainer/manager gives the information, instructs them in what they should do, and the students in general passively and some would say 'blindly' follow instructions— like a programmed computer. Finally they are 'passively' assessed.

Although the use of work-related material and hands on experience helps improve understanding, this authoritarian approach has a dramatic effect on the trainee, and the learning process is still largely blocked. The outcome, therefore, is essentially the continuation of surface learning depicted above for the traditional lecture approach.

Two-way enquiry

The greatest understanding of knowledge and how to apply it, *whatever the subject area*, is achieved through a two-way *collaborative* group approach, where the trainer/manager allows and encourages students/ trainees to e.g.:

- reflect together on the issues being considered
- input and build on their own experiences and perspectives
- openly question information and theory
- discuss and weigh up differing viewpoints and evidence
- challenge accepted views and opinions (including the trainer's), as a

basis for continuous change of course content (particularly in the case of experienced employees closest to the process)
- present reasoned argument and suggest different approaches
- make decisions (e.g. on choice of projects and assignments)
- teach
- give and receive feedback
- be involved in their own assessment (self-team assessment is an integral part of a collaborative team approach considered in Chapter 12).

This collaborative interaction is central to effective learning and has a powerful effect on students/trainees. By allowing them to reflect and talk about what they think is going on, and take part in assessing their own progress, etc., knowledge becomes part of them rather than something external and separate. This ensures that the learning process and related activities are relevant to them as people, and not just to the workplace. It is key to building interest and self-confidence, and binding people to learning and workplace activities. In turn, it highly motivates students, trainees and employees to learn and find out more.

Encourage recording Students/trainees should be encouraged to write things down *in their own words* after group meetings. This is a valuable tool for learning and helps to:

- cement and enhance their knowledge and understanding
- organize and clarify their thoughts
- encourage and fix new ideas which can be inputted into the next group meeting.

Note Remove all fear of writing (created in the traditional educational and working environments), by explaining that, for the time being:

- spelling words wrongly does not matter
- using the wrong grammar does not matter
- OK to use drawings and diagrams if you are unable, or find it difficult, to use words
- getting things 100 per cent correct is not necessary.

(See also Chapter 12.)

Once the fear of being judged is removed, and writing things down is seen purely as an aid for working out and recording views and ideas, the trainee's inhibitions will be removed. Also, the incentive to improve and if necessary get remedial help, will be greatly increased. The use of word processors and audio-video packages are effective facilitators of this process. The same situation exists for the use of mathematics.

Core teaching skills By fully involving people in the process of enquiry, critical thinking and decision-making, therefore, it encourages them to identify more closely with, and be committed to, the work. As was considered in earlier chapters in the context of employees in the workplace, it facilitates the development of team-learning skills essential for continuous and fully effective learning. This is as true for the teacher as the student (see also Chapter 9).

Central to enquiry-based learning is a trainer who has, or is developing, the core collaborative attitudes and skills (Figure 4.1). As a minimum, students/trainees need to know that they will be listened to; and if they have got something wrong, the trainer/manager will talk about it and encourage the group to talk about it, rather than criticize or (encourage) ridicule. Otherwise, involvement, enquiry, and learning will be blocked.

> The core attitudes and skills of effective teaching/training are one and the same as the core attitudes and skills of effective teamwork, learning and leadership.

Group learning   The beneficial effect of group learning is reflected in the following typical remarks by trainees/students:

It's not just sitting there getting bored, it's participating as well, and being able to make mistakes and not get crucified.

We have found as a group that the weak ones are being helped by the stronger ones, so it's a good learning experience for everybody.

The tutor listens and does not point the finger; if you've got it wrong you will talk about it and you don't laugh at each other.

We learn probably as much by the discussions in groups as we do by what we have been taught and what we have read.

People see things from different angles, so it makes it easier to understand by discussing and working in groups.

There's a high level of challenge and critical evaluation, it's a powerful learning vehicle.

> A collaborative group approach in which the trainer/manager encourages a climate of listening and dialogue, without judgement or ridicule, ensures interest—a key motivater—and incentive for students to apply the tools of writing and mathematics.

Collaborative working cultures   As considered in Chapter 5, whether or not a trainer/manager can fully develop and deploy collaborative attitudes and skills is dependent on them being part of a collaborative organizational culture. This is the case whether the teacher is internal or external.

A switch from hierarchically to collaboratively run institutions both on the part of external training providers—colleges, universities and private providers—and industry, is essential for fully implementing the following interdependent situations:

- Partnership dialogue between external providers and industry, ensuring that providers listen and respond to the needs of employers and employees.
- Partnership dialogue between external teachers and students/ trainees, enabling full student involvement in the learning process, ensuring relevance, interest, motivation, and effective learning.

Due to the core skills involved, a collaboratively run company is more likely to develop an effective partnership with external training providers than the traditional hierarchical organization (e.g. the Nissan example above).

Fully cost-effective training is only achievable through a collaborative approach between trainer and customer, teacher and learner, which enables the greatest understanding of knowledge and ability/motivation to apply it i.e. skill competence.

Example　In response to the challenge posed by Asia's manufacturing explosion, and convinced that employees' skills are critical for a company's survival, John Neill, chief executive of the car parts group Unipart, directed large funds to the building of an in-house university. The university aims to bring continuous learning to employees to help counter not just low cost but also increasingly high tech competition from the East.[2]

In contrast to traditional universities, 'Unipart U' is open to all employees in the Group, not just a privileged few such as management. (This also runs counter to the elitist approach still prevalent in industry, where management and supervisory training generally exceeds training for operatives, sales staff and technicians.) In contrast to traditional training, and as mentioned in the previous chapter, there are no exams or degrees and no pass or fail, but knowledge learned in courses is expected to be taken away and used immediately in the workplace. In line with points made in this chapter, courses are directly related to the workplace, and incorporate hands-on experience for the student in situations which simulate workplace activities.

Also in line with this chapter, courses aim to be collaborative through the following two routes. Firstly, through encouraging a non-authoritarian equal-footing approach by enabling all employees to be either student or teacher depending on whether they are trying to learn new skills or teach their own skills to others. The second route is through facilitating debate in the classroom and encouraging students to challenge the teacher with views drawn from their own experience. This input from employees closest to the job is seen as a basis for continuously updating the structure and content of courses, and also possibly influencing company policy and investment decisions. Attempt to effect the latter route to collaborative training is indicated by the comment of a course leader. At the beginning of a day's session to teach the theory of Just in Time as applied to practice, he makes the following request in order to improve the value of the day, i.e., the extent of their learning:

We're going to talk about the Toyota production system. So what I want you to do throughout the course of the day is to actually talk to each other in a structured way of course through myself, ask questions. The quality of the debate will give you a good value day.

Overcoming the traditional training approach

Traditional hierarchical attitudes and behaviours, as has been considered, are deeply rooted, and reversing these cannot be done merely by requesting people to behave differently either in the workplace or on training courses. For instance, there was great improvement over the traditional approach in the course referred to in the above example, in that it fulfilled two out of the three conditions considered above for effective training, i.e. it was work-related and hands-on. However, it appeared not to give prominence to the third requirement, i.e. for training to be collaborative. For example, the hands-on part of the training, which was in the form of a game, appeared mainly to concentrate on applying a system (Kanban, Just in Time), rather than on how people were relating. Certainly, trainees were better able to master the theory of the new system and work more as a team through the practical activity of the game, which served to reveal confusions and misunderstandings about the theory, and enable progress to a more orderly application of it. However, the exercise appeared to be undertaken within a framework where traditional hierarchical (non-collaborative) interactions remained intact. The group, therefore, illustrated certain of the characteristics of a 'hierarchical team' and the core interpersonal attitudes and skills that underpin it (Chapters 4 and 5). For example, some trainees made adversarial, confrontational and judgemental statements, not merely during the confusion stage, but also towards the end of the game. One trainee, for instance, possibly role playing a plant manager, shouted abrasively: 'Seven, finished product please, now!—Just in time!'.

There is no question that the above referred to course is highly superior to traditional training, and the company have great success with it. Also, the above exercise was in the form of a game, and there is no doubt that an element of fun and humour facilitates learning. Any qualification on the basis of interpersonal interactions, therefore, might appear to be nit-picking. The point being made earlier in this and in subsequent chapters, however, is that it is essential to go one step further and to integrate fully a collaborative approach into training, centred on corresponding core interpersonal attitudes and skills (Chapter 4), in order to:

- Enable the *deepest* understanding of knowledge and how to apply it, needed for fully effective and cost-effective training.
- Model *reciprocal* manager-employee-supplier-customer relationships which are of paramount importance for success in the workplace.

This requires a definite structure and framework to training, as will be considered in Chapter 10.

Summary: the two main reasons why training courses are often a waste of money

1 *The traditional hierarchical culture of training providers*
This leads them arrogantly to offer off-the-shelf academic courses, and prevents them from working in partnership with employers and employees to provide flexible, work-related, hands-on, collaborative training.

2 *The traditional hierarchical culture of the workplace*

(a) This leads training/managers to send people to irrelevant off-the-shelf courses.

(b) In-house courses run by these organizations, while likely to be more work-related and possibly hands-on, are not likely to be collaborative.

(c) Even if external training courses endeavour to be work-related, hands-on and collaboratively involve the student, a traditional, hierarchical working culture will block off an effective partnership with the course providers, and the knowledge and skills trainees gain from such courses will not be fully utilized and extended within the workplace.

These two reasons why training courses are often ineffective and wasteful, apply to any kind of training, whether it is technical skills training or communication/team/management skills training.

Note Examples of companies and training providers who have attempted to move away from the traditional approach indicate just how resilient hierarchical attitudes are to change. This is illustrated for example by the now widespread team-leadership management training course. Despite the appearance of being practical and relevant, persisting hierarchical attitudes have meant that such courses tend to maintain an overly theoretical component and to create artificial team activities, which fail to equip the trainee with procedures which can be integrated effectively into workplace activities (e.g. example Chapter

10). This represents a tremendous and continuing waste of resources.

Exercise   Assess how much the training approaches used in your organization meet the three criteria: work-related, hands-on, collaborative.

Notes   1. Some changes have been made along these lines, prompted by the Government, with the realization that it will not be possible to develop and complete higher NVQ levels (4 and 5) on the existing approach to levels 1 to 3. So far, however, the changes have been limited and fragmentary, and more radical alterations will be required.
2. Information and quotation taken from videotape of Unipart University launch, 1993. The interpretations are this author's.

Reference   Smithers A. (1993). *All Our Futures: Britain's Education Revolution*, a report of the Channel 4 Commission on Education. Produced for Channel 4 by Broadcasting Support Services in association with the Centre for Education and Employment Research, University of Manchester (Channel 4 Television, London).

9 Core transferable skills

Chapters 4, 5 and 8 considered the core collaborative attitudes and skills common to effective teamwork, learning, leadership and teaching/training. This chapter will consider how these core attitudes and skills are central to all areas of skill development and training.

Artificial division of skills

Skills are often separated into the following broad categories:

- technical skills
- financial skills
- people skills.

In turn, *people skills* are separated into categories such as:

- − communication skills
- − influencing skills/intervention skills
- − team skills

Under this kind of labelling, managers for example would be considered to need financial and people skills, whereas scientists, engineers and technicians would be considered to need mainly technical skills.

Confusing skills

It should be realized, however, that this separation of skills is artificial, and it can be highly confusing. For example, a handbook for students in one college of Higher Education bombards students with the following array of skills they need to develop:

Study skills and transferable skills—key areas:

Communication skills
Group and interpersonal skills
Organization and personal skills
Research and problem-solving skills
Information technology skills
Numerical skills

Other skills referred to under the above include:

note-taking skills
oral expression skills
written expression skills
writing skills
discussion skills
presentation skills
evaluation skills
interpretation skills

Confusingly, 'working in groups', 'listening and communication skills' and 'handling numerical data', are initially indicated under 'communication skills'; whereas later 'communication skills', 'group and interpersonal skills', and 'numerical skills 'are split up and considered separately. Also, 'discussion skills' are only referred to under 'communication skills' but not under 'group skills'; 'presentation skills' are referred to under both 'communication skills' and 'numerical skills' but only these; 'evaluation skills' are referred to under 'research and problem-solving skills' only; and 'analyzing skills' are referred to under 'organizational and personal skills' and 'research and problem-solving skills' only, etc. If the students were not confused before, they are likely to be after this kind of consideration.

Although it is convenient to separate out different kinds of skills, it is often overdone, and generally it misleads people into believing that there are distinct sets of skills. It belies the fact that the variously labelled skills are inextricably linked and rooted in the same core skills, as shall be considered below.

Artificial division of mental and practical

There is the further separation of skills into practical and mental or intellectual skills. Technician skills, catering skills, bricklaying skills, for example, are considered to be practical or mainly practical skills, whereas accounting skills, management skills, legal skills, teaching skills, and scientific skills, etc., are classed as intellectual or mainly intellectual skills. This is a purely artificial separation. It stems from an elitist hierarchical culture which has traditionally separated theory from practice (see for example, Chapter 8), and distinguished between academic and vocational education, giving greatest esteem to theory-loaded education and undervaluing practice-loaded education.

The theory-practice, academic-vocational link

Teaching a practical task—how to do something—without theory or with watered down theory (without considering why), as was considered in the reference to NVQs in the previous chapter, will not produce someone fully competent in the skill. Neither will teaching theory without a practical component: a widespread phenomenon in the educational system, and a key factor undermining the effectiveness of traditional teacher and management training, for example.

When someone undertakes a task effectively, whether it is in the area of plumbing, or management, or whatever, theory and practice, thinking and doing, are inextricably bound together in the action. Therefore:

To develop any skill competently requires a close mental-practical mix, and a developed intellectual element.

The more people develop their thinking skills: questioning, evaluating, predicting, suggesting, etc., the more they will be able to understand the theory and effectively apply it in practice, i.e. the more effective their skills.

Core people skills

Figure 4.1 depicts how discussion and communication skills, etc., are dependent on the skills of consulting, questioning, suggesting, evaluating, etc., which in turn are dependent on core interpersonal attitudes and skills such as respect and listening. These are the skills of interrelating effectively—in short, 'people skills'. Chapters 4, 5 and 8 considered how these various people skills are the basis not only of interrelating effectively in a team, but also of learning effectively (and leading and teaching effectively).

The basis of all learning

Recent research in Britain and America[1] draws attention to the fundamental importance of people skills in the learning process. Much of the research has been prompted by the way in which, in recent years, girls' performance in education has significantly improved and outstripped that of boys. The improved performance has occurred at all levels: primary school, GCSE results, 'A'level results, university graduation results; and over all subjects areas: mathematics, science, technology, geography, history, foreign languages, English.

Cultural male–female differences

The above research cited a difference in *attitude* as a major factor in the difference between male and female performance. Figure 9.1 indicates characteristics in males not generally found in females cited by the various researchers and revealed by comments made by pupils and students; and also some male pupil's comments. Besides findings claimed to indicate biological differences between the brains of the genders from birth, giving females a language and therefore learning advantage, differences in treatment of the sexes by parents was cited as a major cause of the above listed characteristics. This author would add that, in turn, a strong influence on the parents is the prevailing 'macho' hierarchical culture, reflected in social and work environments.

Transferable 'people' skills

According to the above research, therefore, superior communication or 'people' skills in females are the reason for their greatly improved performance compared to males in areas such as technology, mathematics and science, *and not just languages*. Similarly, previous research in the 1970s[2] indicated how a particular group discussion

---

Cultural characteristics of male pupils

---

easily distracted
difficulty in concentrating
poor communication skills
poor skills of presentation
poor skills of expression
poor reading skills
difficulty in listening
individualistic
low level of understanding
arrogant about their brain power
reverence of the 'macho' male
championing of adversarial behaviour
championing of confrontational behaviour
championing of disrespectful behaviour
difficulty in working quietly and cooperatively
difficulty in showing respect to the teacher and others

Comments of male pupils

It's not a macho thing to work.
I think it's really good to get into trouble.
You don't really care.
It's important to stand out.
If you get thrown out of class you impress people, you are a hero.
Boys have got bigger brains [than girls].

Figure 9.1 *Cultural male anti-learning attitudes*

programme led to improvements in areas such as reasoning skills/ critical thinking skills and mathematics.

Significantly, a lack of respect and ability to listen are cited as relevant factors undermining males' performance in the recent research (Table 9.1). Likewise the discussion programme in the earlier research referred to hinged on the development of respect and listening skills. Ultimately, therefore, it is the effect of the national culture to instil in male pupils non-collaborative attitudes such as disrespect and arrogance, which blocks their ability to interrelate cooperatively and effectively with adults (verbally or through reading): to listen to them, take on board ideas, and to develop the skills of consulting, requesting, evaluating, informing, describing, receiving critical feedback, etc. (Figure 4.1), which would enable them to further develop their ideas, imagination and creativity.

Put simply, if a pupil is not able to listen and express themselves to a teacher, then that teacher cannot help them develop their ideas and understanding. (This is not to allocate blame to male pupils. As mentioned above, males are moulded from birth by the prevailing culture, and teachers are part of this culture.)

'People' skills, underpinned by collaborative interpersonal attitudes and skills (Figure 4.1), are the core transferable skills needed for effective learning in all areas.

A collaborative approach which nurtures 'people' skills is the core vehicle for all learning and skill development.

Technical skills through team skills

The more developed the core team or 'people' skills of respect, humility, listening, etc.:

- The more effectively someone will *learn* skills, i.e. understand theory and how to apply it in practice.
- The more competently someone will *apply* skills in a real setting, i.e. the more effective their judgements and decisions in the workplace.

It is possible to develop technical and financial skills in the narrow sense of being able to master academic exercises and techniques in a remote artificial setting. This in fact is what much of academic education has done. However, technical and financial skills in the broad sense of making technical and financial judgements and decisions *in a real setting* will be more effective the more the people skills of respect, listening, consulting, etc., are developed.

A manager, for example, will make more effective financial judgements if he or she consults and acts on the views and development needs of the workforce. Similarly, an engineer will make more effective technical judgements if he or she consults and acts on the views of colleagues, suppliers and customers.

People skills and effective training

It has been considered above that whatever area of skill development a student is embarking on—whether it is in plumbing, engineering, scientific research, teaching, managing, etc.—the student needs to be allowed and encouraged to develop the underpinning core people or team-learning skills (Figure 4.1) in order to learn effectively. *All* training therefore needs to cater for this requirement.

> Training in any area—quality, technical skills, financial skills, etc.—is only fully effective within a framework which develops core people skills

As considered in Chapter 5 and briefly in Chapter 8, this requires the teacher or trainer themselves to have developed (or be in the process of developing) the core people skills.

Overall benefits of people skills for trainers/managers

Trainers/managers with (or in the process of developing) core people skills will improve their competence in three interrelated ways. They will be able to:

1 Learn knowledge and skills (of any kind) more effectively.
2 Apply knowledge and skills more effectively.
3 Work collaboratively with trainees/employees to develop and get the best out of them, tapping their ideas, imagination and creativity as the basis for continuous improvement in efficiency and added-value.

Point 3 will incorporate:

- The trainer/manager involving the trainee/employee in group discussion, problem-solving and decision-making, which:
  - develops trainees' core team-learning skills;
  - facilitates trainees' skill development;
  - enables trainees to challenge trainers' views, facilitating trainers' core learning skills development, and enhancing continuous change and improvement in courses/processes;
  - harnesses trainees' ideas, imagination and creativity to enhance efficiency, quality and innovation in processes and product.
- The trainer/manager facilitating the merging of teacher–learner roles which:
  - enhances the trainers'/managers' opportunities to learn from, adapt to, and harness their trainees' experiences and skills;
  - provides trainees with the opportunity to teach, which:
  (a) motivates them to search for up-to-date information, further developing their learning skills and enhancing their knowledge, skills, and understanding
  (b) exposes them to questioning and feedback from the group, again developing their learning skills, etc.

How these benefits to trainers and managers can be brought about in practice is considered in Chapter 10.

Notes   1. See: *The Assessment of Performance in Design and Technology*, by Richard Kimbell *et al.*, APU Goldsmith's College, SCAA, 1991;

'Gender, Ethnic, and Socio-economic Differences in Attainment and Progress', by Pam Sammons in: *British Educational Research*, Volume 21, 4, 1995; 'The Future is Female', *Panorama*, BBC, October 10, 1994.

2. Cited for example in 'Summary of results of 1976–78 experimental research in philosophy for children: Newark and Pompton Lakes', by Matthew Lipman and V. C. Shipman, *Institute for the Advancement of Philosophy for Children Report*, 1979.

10 A core training and working vehicle

Chapter 9 considered the core transferable skills central to all areas of learning and training. This chapter will consider the use of a training structure which:

- Nurtures the vital core learning (teaching and management) skills
- Can effectively be deployed for all skills training
- Directly models, and therefore can be integrated into, day-to-day activities in the workplace

A structured training–working format

Chapters 8 and 9 considered how training needs to be collaboratively run, so that trainees are able to develop the core 'collaborative' or 'people' skills (Figure 4.1) fundamental to effective learning in all areas. What is required is for the trainer to deploy a *structured procedure* which ensures the simultaneous development and use of the core skills within the training process. Furthermore, because of the requirement that training should be work-related, the training procedure needs to be relevant to workplace needs, and to *model* workplace activities so that it can be integrated effectively into those activities.

The collaborative team format

An approach which satisfies all these requirements is the collaborative team format (Aid 10.1). This core training format can be adapted to various settings in the workplace, and these will be overlapping in a learning organizational culture:

- groupwork/team meetings (shop-floor, inter/departmental, customer–supplier, etc.)
- committee meetings
- board meetings
- selection interviewing
- conflict management
- change management
- staff appraisal.

- **Ask the group to form a 'circle'**
  - if possible with people sitting at tables
- **Agree on ground rules for proceeding**
  - e.g. don't all talk at once, listen to and value what others say or they won't value or listen to you, avoid dominance by one or two members, behave courteously, avoid negative disagreement, avoid personal criticism and point scoring
- **Begin with a brief consideration of the issue to be discussed**
  - presented by team leader or a group member
- **Encourage expression of ideas, beliefs, concerns, solutions, etc.**
  - gather as many views and ideas as possible
- **Visually record**
  - if appropriate appoint someone in the group to write up points (make sure it is legible)
- **Encourage evaluation**
  - counter side-tracks and irrelevancies, frequently summarize
- **Write up group's conclusions and decisions for future action**
  - agree who should undertake the action

Aid 10.1   *The core training–working team format*

In most situations, including trainer/manager training (see below), the 'consideration of material to be discussed' should be as brief as possible. Other skills training, however, might require a more extended consideration of the subject area (see later).

The size of the 'group' may be as little as two. Although it is possible to have groups as big as 30, ideally the maximum is about 20 members, with optimum size between 6 and 15.

Enquiry-based trainer/ manager training

Core skills development
A key skill of trainers/managers, therefore, will be effectively to deploy the above team format, which requires them to have the core people skills (Figure 4.1). Lectures and books on training are full of

instructions/imperatives to trainers and managers to:

discuss	consult	analyse	present
clarify	facilitate	evaluate	listen
enable	share	motivate	etc.

These are valid exhortations. However, in themselves they are unlikely to change practice. They do not tell people *how* to develop and enact these skills. As considered in Chapters 4 and 5, these behaviours ultimately require changes in underlying interpersonal attitudes which have prevailed in the workplace.

People do not develop new skills, and in particular the core people skills and underlying attitudes, merely by being told about them, lectured to about them, or reading about them. Neither will fictional examples and games, contrived exercises and puzzles, or outdoor activities— widespread in trainer/manager training courses—greatly help.

> Artificial team activities, such as contrived exercises, games and outdoor activities, might boost morale in the short-term, but are entirely inappropriate for changing behaviour in the workplace and for tackling deep-rooted attitudes which genuine team development requires.

Aids to practice

As with any other kinds of training, trainer/manager training needs to be work-related, hands-on and collaboratively run. Training in the key people skills, therefore, needs to centre around practising using the core team format (Aid 10.1). This requires the help of two further aids: the *core interpersonal skills checklist* (Aid 10.2), and *open questioning techniques* (Aid 10.3).

Trainer/manager training framework

On the basis of the above, a training scenario for trainers/managers would follow the broad framework indicated in Figure 10.1.

Do I:
- present a relaxed, non-abrasive manner?
- make eye contact and look attentive?
- avoid lecturing?
- avoid compelling people to follow a particular agenda of ideas?
- let people's ideas and understanding emerge from their own interests and dialogue?
- ask open questions to find out people's views?
- patiently give time for people to respond?
- listen attentively to answers without thinking about the person's status, how they look, dress, talk, and what point I am going to make next?
- avoid interrupting and imposing my own views and solutions?
- indicate that what people say makes me think?
- avoid insisting all comments be directed to me/the team leader?
- avoid making personal remarks?
- avoid making judgements against people's ability?
- help to draw out people's views and feelings by reflecting (repeating) their response?
- periodically summarize what has been said to clarify and elicit further response?
- make sure the main points are recorded visually?
- encourage openness by tolerating differing and opposing views?
- ask open questions to:
  - encourage people to appraise their own reasons and assumptions?
  - help people stick to the point?
  - help people be consistent?
  - encourage people to appraise the implications of their own views?
  - encourage people to seek, question and value the views of others?
  - encourage people to evaluate situations and suggest solutions to problems?
- inform and fill in where necessary?
- take criticism constructively without being defensive, contradictory, or apologetic?
- take or delegate action on the basis of decisions reached?

Aid 10.2   *Core interpersonal skills checklist*

To elicit views
　　What are your views on ...?
　　Tell me something about your experience of ...
　　How did you do/feel when ...?
　　Can you explain what you mean a bit more?
　　Are there any more thoughts on that item?

To elicit further views by reflecting and summarizing
　　As I understand you, you're saying that ...
　　So am I correct in believing you are saying ...?

To elicit underlying reasons and assumptions
　　Would you like to say why you think that is so?
　　What is your reason for saying that ...?
　　On what grounds/evidence do you believe that ...?

To help people be consistent and keep to the point
　　I am not clear. Tell me why you think ... is linked with your
　　earlier point?
　　Are you making the same point now as you did earlier when you
　　said ...?

To help people consider the implications of their views
　　So what do you think would be the outcome of what you're
　　suggesting?
　　In view of what you've said, are you implying that?

To encourage a consideration of alternative views
　　Does any one else have a different view on this?
　　What if someone were to suggest that ...?

To encourage appraisal of suggestions and solutions
　　Can I sum up your suggestion/solution as follows ...?
　　Could you give a summary of the points you are making and
　　where you think we should go?

To encourage evaluation of outcomes
　　How would you describe what happened?
　　How do you think you did?
　　Why do you think that happened?
　　How would you make changes/tackle the problem?
　　(Use some of the questioning under the above headings to fully
　　evaluate the ideas, beliefs and suggestions brought up.)

Aid 10.3　*Examples of open questions*

1
Trainer-led group session modelling the team format (Aid 10.1) To consider its use as a core learning-working vehicle. (Begin with brief exposition of: the core attitudes and skills of teamwork, leadership and learning (Fig. 4.1); the team format, interpersonal skills checklist and open questioning techniques (Aids 1, 2 and 3); and how the Aids are to be used to facilitate core skills development (see below and Chapter 12).)
2
Trainer-led group session modelling the team format To consider a real work-related topic.
3
Trainee-led group sessions practising the team format To consider their own work-related issues. (Time set aside towards the end of the session to allow for group feedback on the performance of the trainee leader.)

Figure 10.1   *Training framework for trainer/manager training*

Use of aids   Ideally every trainee would have the opportunity to lead a session. The same core skills (and attitudes), however, are developed by the experience of participating as a group member. Therefore, the aids should be used continually by all trainees in the group as follows:

1 By each trainee as a guide before a session.
2 By each trainee to assess their own behaviour against them as soon as possible after a session.
3 By the whole group during a session to give feedback to the trainee who has led the session.

1 and 3 are more effective than 2, particularly at the beginning of this kind of training when the skill of self-appraisal is poorly developed. Generally it is difficult to be objective about one's own behaviour, and an aspect of developing a collaborative working approach is to increase self-appraisal skills. Therefore, although the use of checklists, the Aids 10.1, 10.2 and 10.3, by individuals is an important part of the learning process, initially they are probably more effective as a guide before a session than as a means of accurately assessing behaviour after a session. On the other hand, open feedback from the group is highly effective and can be highly supportive (see Chapter 12 for a general consideration of feedback, evaluation and appraisal).

No quick fix magic formula

The core skills and attitudes which need to be developed in trainers/ managers for them effectively to deploy the team format (Aid 10.1) cannot be developed overnight. It often requires changing the habits and attitudes of a lifetime, and it is not possible to apply any of the above three aids to a formula. Initially individuals will be unable to use Aid 10.2 fully effectively for themselves before core attitudes and skills such as humility and self-appraisal are developed. Similarly, it is unlikely that individuals will have the respect, trust and ability to listen, etc. to be able to use open questions (Aid 10.3) in a genuine manner. The aids, however, are useful guides for structured action on which changes in attitudes and skill improvement can be built through group feedback and continued use (see below and Chapter 12).

> **Give time** It is important that trainers make clear to trainee trainers/managers that a 3-day or even a 10-week course should be viewed as a springboard for continuing development in the workplace.

Barriers to deploying the team format

The main barriers to a trainee trainer/manager learning effectively to deploy the collaborative team format are:

1 Ingrained hierarchical attitudes
2 The working culture they return to after training.

Barrier 1 Ingrained hierarchical attitudes

Trainee trainers/managers are likely to fall prey to two main practical stumbling blocks as a result of ingrained hierarchical attitudes (Figure 5.2), which cannot be shaken off easily.

The hierarchical 'skill' of talking rather than listening

This is endemic among trainers and managers, and linked with a tendency to be abrasive, judgemental, intolerant, insincere, inconsistent, etc., and an inability to self-appraise. It is rooted in disrespect and distrust in other people's views and abilities, and an arrogant belief in one's own superior knowledge and abilities.

As a result, the trainee trainer/manager is likely to spend too much of the session they lead (Figure 10.1) by talking, giving more of a lecture on the subject area than a 'brief consideration'. They will find it difficult to be silent, to hang back, to elicit and listen to the views of others, before rushing in and giving their own views, evaluations and decisions. This is highly discouraging for team members/learners. It greatly undermines their self-esteem, devalues their ideas, and demotivates their will to participate constructively.

Trainers should also warn against:

- Beginning a group meeting handing down decisions that have already been made higher up the hierarchy.
- Handing out typed sheets giving views and decisions made by people up the hierarchy, and asking for the group's comments:
  - often used as a ploy to give the semblance of group involvement; equally as inhibiting and demotivating as openly imposed views and decisions; and counterproductive, as team members will perceive it as dishonest and manipulative, increasing distrust and cynicism.

The tendency to overcompensate for a judgemental hierarchical approach

This arises from the belief that it is possible to encourage participation by giving a great deal of praise. Traditionally this has been a hazard of teachers and trainers more than managers, but could become so for managers as they increasingly take on a training/coaching role. Praise is important and everybody needs it but reacting to group members' responses with too many 'yesses' and 'goods' is ineffective. It can inhibit alternative views, and becomes just as judgemental and trainer- or manager-centred as the traditional non-listening hierarchical approach.

Overcoming stumbling blocks

The ability to overcome the above stumbling blocks and effectively to deploy the core training-working team format will be developed in trainers/managers through the following main experiences:

- Participation as a team member in an experienced trainer-led session during a course.
- Feedback from team members when leading a session during a training course.
- Experience of leading a session with a group back in the workplace (this on-going learning is potentially the main learning experience—see later and Chapter 12).

Barrier 2 The trainee's workplace culture

The second barrier to deploying the team format effectively is the working culture the trainee returns to. However effective a course might be in initiating collaborative team skills development, if the trainee returns to a traditional hierarchical organization, he or she will not be able effectively to deploy and continue to develop these skills. There would need to be a (developing) collaborative culture, reflected in a horizontal structure along the lines indicated in Chapter 6, which:

- has teams in place throughout the organization
- expects managers/trainers to deploy a collaborative team approach and encourages them by recognizing and supporting them on that basis
- encourages and rewards (recognizes and supports) all employees on a team involvement basis
- has no judgemental appraisal systems blocking openness, listening, etc. and learning (see also Chapter 12).

It follows that if such a structure is not in place, or not in the process of being developed, then managers/trainers who have attended training courses will find it difficult to implement what they have been taught for the following reasons:

- It will be marginal to their own and their teams' rewards, and generally they will not feel supported to participate in and develop a team approach.
- Juniors will be cynical and untrusting to them about the genuineness of the approach and fear being open, etc.
- They will be cynical and untrusting to their superiors about the genuineness of the approach and fear being open, etc.

If one adds to this work-culture barrier the fact that much leadership-team training, although it might bring about some increase in group discussion and listening between trainees (other managers/trainers), often does not give a structured framework which the trainee can take back to the workplace, then the chances of such training being ineffective is very high.

If money on leadership-team training is not to be wasted, it needs to be an integral part of implementing and developing a collaborative learning culture (see Chapters 11 and 12).

Example: training vs 'the old ways of doing things'

A top manager (CEO) who *talks* about the need to empower people will not empower people; and trainers who *talk* about the ways in which people learn, will not help people learn. This was illustrated in the case of an expensive in-house training programme for middle managers, using external trainers, in one large Euro-American company.[1]

According to a senior manager, the aim of the training programme was to develop middle managers' ability to empower people to make decisions and act upon their own intelligence. The training programme consisted of a 1-week course, and a follow-up 6 months later with feedback (including feedback from juniors in the workplace).

During the course

One manager (A) referred to the way working in teams on the course had changed members, and how they had become much more participative and helped each other solve problems, listen to each other, and become more focused on the way they were working. He began to realize that he did not do much to encourage his small team back at work to look at the job, the way that it is done and the processes used. Although he felt he was sympathetic in terms of understanding what they are doing, he acknowledged he was 'fairly directive', and not good at giving them guidance or helping them consider, with him, whether the job could be done better and the processes improved.

Similarly, a second manager (B), who felt that his team back at work had very good morale and team spirit, said he was conscious that he sets the goals and direction and just tells people to 'get out and do it'. He was aware that he probably fell short of the course's prescription to be sensitive, approachable, open and fair.

After the course　Manager A referred to his plan to give presentations to people on future plans, so as to make himself more active in 'trying to sell people my ideas'. Manager B said that he was getting out more and had restructured the way he planned his week, which he thought probably occurred as a result of attending the course.

Neither manager referred to any attempt to move away from their self-confessed directive approach. Later, in the context of responding to feedback from his work team 6 months later, manager B said that he had been trying to move away from the traditional goal-orientated management approach, controlling, routinizing, structuring, formulating, to a more open approach encouraging a lot more responsibility by people for their job and what they do. He expressed surprise and disappointment when, as he saw it, the feedback questionnaire indicated that his team wanted the former approach—more control, etc., and a more hierarchical structure—in their department.

Conclusion on the course　Despite great expense, the course failed to begin to make significant inroads on 'the old ways of doing things'. In line with the points made earlier in this section, this is not surprising given the following facts:

- Although the trainees were told about how people learn and the importance of empowerment, and they experienced team working and discussion during the course, they were not given a structured framework which they could take back and apply within workplace activities to support them to continue to develop learning and empower their teams.
- Despite senior management rhetoric on the central importance of empowerment, there were no corresponding structural changes to support team learning and empowerment on the ground, and no example set from the top (see Chapter 12).

Morals for trainers

> Telling people (theories) about how they learn will not help them learn.

The prevailing management/trainer training course which e.g. focuses on styles of learning, team roles, unstructured team discussion, contrived management games, or outdoor activities, fails to provide, and give practice in, a suitable practical procedure for day-to-day activities in the workplace.

Morals for top managers

Telling people you are empowering them will not empower them, unless you start *acting* to change the organization's structure and culture (see Chapter 12).

Isolated training for middle managers in aspects of TQM—teamworking, empowerment, involvement, customer care (internal and external) etc.—will be largely money down the drain.

Continuing workplace learning

The ideal characteristic of the above training framework (Figure 10.1) is that it directly models the activities of the trainees in the workplace—group meetings, departmental meetings, interviews, etc.,—and therefore can be taken back and directly used and practised in the workplace (assuming the culture is right). Initially, as the attitudes of respect, humility, honesty, etc., and corresponding skills such as listening and self-appraisal are poorly developed, the developing trainer/manager will not be able to deploy the team format fully effectively. However, the continued use of the above learning aids will begin to develop the underlying attitudes. Merely going through the process of acting out the procedures in Aid 10.1, asking people for their comments and ideas, and visually recording them, can produce a positive response in team members, even though at first the trainer/manager might find it difficult *genuinely* to listen and to value the ideas suggested. A positive and intelligent response by team members, however, will begin to increase the team leader's respect and trust in people, which in turn will produce an even more positive response from team members. There will be a reinforcing cycle. As the ability to deploy the core skills and team format increases, team feedback will also increase, further enhancing the development process.

Trainer/manager training follow-up

Because of the importance of organizational culture, there should be a close partnership between organizations and external trainers. Ideally, training of employed trainer/manager trainees should be part of culture change implementation and building throughout their organization (Chapters 11 and 12). Failing this, the onus is on external trainers to:

- Avoid promoting quality, team and leadership programmes within hierarchical institutions.
- Communicate that team-leadership training for isolated groups of employees, undertaken independently of a complete culture change programme, is at best an expensive tinkering on the margins and at worst can reinforce and exacerbate cynicism and poor performance.
- Strongly voice the paramount need to tackle hierarchical attitudes and 'skills' at the tops of organizations as the key prerequisite of effective culture change.

At the very minimum, follow-up should be an integral part of external training. The trainer would need to go into the workplace to observe and give feedback to trainee trainers/managers a number of weeks after the course, and then some months later. If the group is large and from different organizations this may not be feasible. Alternatively, the group could meet a few weeks and then a few months later, to give feedback on their experience of applying and developing the core format and skills.

In addition to dispelling any belief in a magic formula 'quick fix' training event, it is also vital that trainers make it clear that the success of team-leadership training (which should be integrated into all management/trainer training), is dependent on the organizational culture which the trainee is (or will become) part of.

Enquiry-based skills training: a general framework

The above framework suggested for effective trainer/manager training (Figure 10.1) closely corresponds to the following general framework found to be effective for practical skills training (Joyce and Showers, 1980):

1 Initial theoretical input: presentation of theory or description of skill or strategy.
2 Practical demonstration in a real situation to follow 1 immediately.
3 Opportunity for trainees to practise in a real setting.
4 Constructive feedback to 3 with coaching.

This is represented diagrammatically in Figure 10.2.

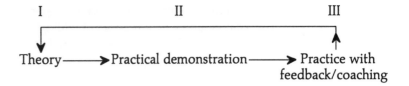

Figure 10.2　*A general training framework*

Conformance of the trainer/manager training framework (Figure 10.1), to the above general training framework is illustrated by Figure 10.3.

General training framework (Fig. 10.2)	Trainer/manager training (Fig. 10.1)
Theory input I	Trainer-led session (1) (also simultaneously a practical demonstration of core skills/team format)
Practical demonstration II	Trainer-led session (2)
Practice with feedback III	Trainee-led sessions (3) (follow-up workplace experience with feedback)

Figure 10.3　*Conformance of trainer/manager training to the general framework*

Collaborative training framework

The general training framework (Figure 10.2) is an improvement over the traditional training approach which relied mainly on a didactic lecture approach. In it the trainee is not just told things, but also *shown* what to do and given the chance to *practise* it in a real situation with feedback and coaching from the trainer. However, it is possible to undertake each stage of the general training framework (Figure 10.2) in an authoritarian manner. That is, each stage would be a one-way top-down process. The initial theory input would comprise a didactic lecture approach, and no stages would enable and encourage questioning or input from the trainee.

According to the message of this book, to be effective, each stage of the training process needs to be undertaken collaboratively. For example, in the case of trainer/manager training considered above, each stage follows the team format allowing trainees to interact collaboratively, questioning, suggesting, deciding, etc.

Furthermore, if undertaken collaboratively, it is ensured that the process is not one-way and static but continuously adapting and updating through trainee involvement and feedback (considered in Chapters 8 and 9). Collaborative training, therefore, would be better represented by adapting the general framework (Figure 10.2) to Figure 10.4.

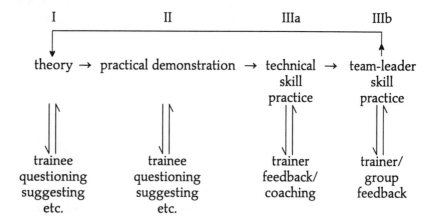

IIIb — gives further theory input
— incorporates trainee project work and assignments

Figure 10.4 *Collaborative 'enquiry-based' training framework*

Collaborative training framework

Re trainer/manager training

Stages I and II: these can be combined.

Stage IIIa: this refers to the use of machinery/equipment, and is not applicable.

All stages follow the team format (Aid 10.1).

Traditional management training

Consideration of a series of topics relating to financial and operational techniques, systems and processes, where the topics of leadership and teamwork are *added on* to the list.

Collaborative management training

Consideration of a series of topics relating to financial and operational techniques, systems, and processes, *within a framework which simultaneously develops* the key management skills of leadership and teamwork.

The same contrast can be made for trainer/teacher training.

Re technical training   *Stage I*: this follows the team format (Aid 10.1), although the 'consideration of material to be discussed' would probably need to be more extensive. Trainee participation and questioning should be encouraged at all times, even during the consideration of the theory if this lasts more than 10 minutes, and certainly as much time as possible should be set aside afterwards to encourage trainee questioning, suggesting and evaluation.

Stage II: this refers to the trainer demonstrating a technique involving the use of equipment. It should ideally follow the team format, eliciting trainee questioning, etc.

Stage IIIa: this refers to the trainee practising a technique involving the use of equipment, in a real setting (either in the workplace or a simulated workplace setting). It will not follow the team format, although it should be a two-way process, allowing questioning, etc. from the trainee as well as feedback and coaching from the trainer

Stage IIIb: this allows trainees to practise team-leadership skills, and provides a forum for them to present additional ideas and theory, and discuss project work. In addition to enhancing learning, this will support project work and facilitate the writing up of assignments. Trainees should be encouraged to follow the team format in their presentation, and the model of the trainer in stages I and II will be instrumental in encouraging this. However, the level of introspection on the team format (and use of Aids 10.2 and 10.3) will not be as great as in the case of trainer/manager training.

Parallel training and workplace activities

Trainer/manager training   All stages I/II and IIIb directly model the various team meetings/presentations that the trainee will be involved in at work.

Technical training   Stages I and IIIb directly model team meetings/presentations in which the trainee will be expected to be involved in the workplace. Stages II and IIIa directly model two-way practical activities on the shop-floor.

Summary

The above training structure can be used effectively to equip trainees in any discipline, with the core transferable learning-team skills. This gives them self-esteem and confidence to interrelate competently, and continuously to improve skills, processes, and products. As considered in this and previous chapters, to enable these key skills the other side of the equation needs to be a collaborative working culture. The next and final two chapters consider key aspects of implementing and building such a culture in practice.

Note   1. Information and quotations from: 'Learning from Experience',
          Business Matters, BBC, 13 August 1992. The interpretations are this
          author's.

Reference   Joyce B. and Showers B. (1980). 'Improving in-service training: the
          message of research', *Educational Leadership*, Volume 37, pp. 379–385.

11 Implementing a learning culture for quality, innovation and long-term success

This book has considered the competitive case for knowledge and skills, and fundamental aspects of the need for organizations to change from the traditional hierarchical to a collaborative 'learning' culture in order to fully harness and continuously extend knowledge and skills.

This penultimate chapter looks at the example of a Western company which has gone part way to developing a learning culture to illustrate:

- The prevailing difficulty Western managers have in understanding the true nature of the culture change needed, and the central significance of interpersonal skills in that change
- An inadequacy in Western TQM philosophy which has been part of quality culture misperceptions and implementation difficulties
- The four conditions that have to be met in order fully and as quickly as possible to implement a learning culture.

The lessons of TQ implementation

While talk about total quality (TQ) management, and related techniques such as employee involvement and empowerment, single status, customer care, etc., became commonplace by the end of the 1980s, its effective implementation in Western companies remained limited. For example, according to one piece of research (Kearney, 1991), 80 per cent of all TQ initiatives in British companies failed to produce tangible results. Despite this, those failing were reported to have continued with their programmes, and 50 per cent actually viewed them as successful.

Implementation framework

Those Western companies which have had most success in implementing a TQ programme adhere to the following broad framework:

1 A recognition by the top manager of the need to change the traditional hierarchical culture, and develop a more horizontal team

structure involving every employee throughout the organization.
2 Full commitment and active involvement at top management level.
3 An action programme for all employees starting with the CEO.

However, even the 'successful' companies generally claim that there cannot be a 'quick fix', and often acknowledge that after 5 to 10 years they still have not completed the culture change process. Their experiences, in fact, reveal a fourth prerequisite that needs to be added to the above framework, in order fully and as quickly as possible, to implement a learning culture

Implementation of TQ: a representative example

Xerox numbers among those Western companies that have had greatest success in implementing a TQ programme, leading to top quality awards. As considered in Chapter 3, the company responded to superior competition in a manner which satisfied the three conditions of the above implementation framework. However, like many other such companies, it has fallen short of the full implementation of a TQ or learning culture, and its experiences point to a missing fourth condition. It should be stressed, however, that this company is not picked out as an example because its shortcomings have exceeded those in other 'successful' companies, and generally they are widely representative. Furthermore, as will be indicated, not only are many of the shortcomings openly recognized by management, and steps being taken to overcome them to grow a learning culture, but also in large part, they have been encouraged by an inadequacy in Western TQ philosophy and rhetoric.

The company's response to superior competition began in the early 1980s with a 3-day training programme initiated by the then CEO, which was extended to all employees, including the CEO. It focused on[1]:

- quality
- customer satisfaction
- family groups
- teams.

The main areas of training related to:

1 quality improvement processes
2 problem solving
3 interactive skills (with a view to running meetings more appropriately)

Anyone joining the company is still expected to undergo this training.

The consideration of interactive skills is in the form of a separate 'add-on', and takes up approximately 15–20 per cent of the course time towards the end of the course. The main emphasis is on 1 and 2, involving training in:

- quality concepts
- quality language
- quality tools.

Prevailing perceptions of managers

The manner in which the training has been undertaken understandably has led to conceptual confusions. Misconceptions by practising managers about the true nature of the culture change needed to maximize efficiency and added-value is revealed by the following.

Exercise: The rhetoric-action gap 1

Compare the following views based on the comments of a training manager at Rank Xerox, with the 'official' TQ philosophy in a company document and a general publication. Note the different emphasis given, and the way the word 'culture' is used with different meanings. As you read through, note down what you believe are the main differences in outlook.

Training manager

The culture change, the real culture change, was to make customer satisfaction an effective number one priority for the business.

Training was about changing the culture from the outset.

No one was exempted from the training nor are they today. The objective is to give employees the tools, concepts and language of making the culture change a reality.

Quality tools empower people to do something about quality with their managers.

I would not draw a linkage between the more horizontal team structure and *quality* as a *primary* linkage.

I do not think quality as developed in Xerox and Rank Xerox was in the first instance about numbers of layers of management and kinds of managers. I think it was about culture change.

The reduction in number of managers and management layers should be thought of in separate terms in Rank Xerox and Xerox rather than as part of quality.

Producing a less vertical, flatter structure has been to reduce costs, and is a separate and quite discrete initiative [from quality].

In general we do not expect our managers to be trainers.

Wherever we can introduce greater levels of empowerment then we press on ... It is understanding what it means, and understanding how to introduce it—those are the challenges.

Official TQ philosophy

Company document

We support [our quality programme] with quality principles, with quality tools and with management action and behaviour.

We were starting a revolution that not every manager was to survive and that would begin to transform the role of the manager.

At the heart of the changes that had to be made was changing from a hierarchical, functional (vertical) command and control organization to a much more cross functional (horizontal) and participative organization.

Employee involvement and participative problem-solving are absolutely essential for improving quality.

The training was aimed at empowering Rank Xerox employees, vesting them with authority over day-to-day work decisions.

To both enable and facilitate this change the role of the manager had to move from one of director and inspector of results to that of a teacher, coach, facilitator and inspector of the process.

It is up to management to provide leadership by ... establishing and reinforcing a management style of openness, trust, respect, patience and discipline and by creating an environment where everyone can be responsible for quality.

General publication

Empowerment requires flatter organizations with shorter communication paths. In this environment a TQ programme is more likely to succeed.

Significant improvements in quality, customer service, costs, etc., are not possible without employee involvement.

Successful total quality management companies have focused the hearts and minds of all their employees on meeting customer needs. They achieved this transformation by creating a new equality and respect in the workplace by ... fostering teamwork, by giving the front-line workforce more authority to take decisions and by redefining the role of management from planning and control to leadership and support[2].

Common management misunderstandings 1

The main differences between the two outlooks represented above, i.e. the beliefs down on the ground vs TQ philosophy, occur in:

- The perception of culture change and how people are empowered.
- The significance of a horizontal team structure to quality.
- The significance of the role of the manager.

The example illustrates the general situation which prevails in Anglo-Saxon organizations. It is highly representative of just how difficult it is to make the transition in practice, even for those companies that have begun over 10 years to make changes to the traditional culture, and achieved improved performance from this.

The gap between TQ rhetoric and perceptions 'down on the ground'

Concept	Meaning
TQ perceptions on the ground	
Culture change	making customer satisfaction (internal and external), the number one priority.
Employee empowerment	enabled through training in the tools of quality.
	(still a challenge to understand what it means and how to introduce it).
TQ philosophy and rhetoric	
Culture change	going from a hierarchical, vertical, command and control organization to a cross-functional horizontal, participative organization.
Employee empowerment	enabled by culture change.
	incorporating changing the manager's role from controller/inspector to teacher/ coach/ facilitator; creating equality, respect, trust, openness, patience; fostering teamwork giving front-line employees authority to take work decisions and focus on meeting customer needs.

Figure 11.1   *The gap between TQ rhetoric and perceptions on the ground*

can be summarized by Figure 11.1. More fully, the prevailing perception by practitioners is:

- A surface view of culture change—namely 'making customer satisfaction the number one priority'—which does not go deeper into the need for a fundamental change in relationships (and organizational structure) for achieving this priority.
- An overestimation of the effect of training in quality tools, processes and systems, for empowering employees to deliver improved quality and performance.

Training people in quality tools, etc., does not *empower* them to deliver quality

---

Inadequate TQM philosophy

In large part, this persisting view is re-enforced by a TQ philosophy and rhetoric in Western culture which fails to address fully underlying factors that are essential for achieving the rhetoric, and for countering traditional hierarchical attitudes. In particular, within the rhetoric there is:

- An underestimation of the importance of *genuine* teamwork, in which managers develop reciprocal (equal-footing, horizontal, collaborative) relationships with employees in order fully to empower the latter to deliver improved quality and performance.
- A marginalization, and lack of full analysis, of the 'soft' interpersonal attitudes and skills needed to create reciprocal management–employee relationships, and how to develop them.
- A lack of understanding of the key need for CEOs to develop 'soft' interpersonal attitudes and skills for achieving culture change, and the horizontal structure (see Chapter 6) required to support it.

The rhetoric–action gap 2

By investing heavily in R&D, Xerox created the right environment to unleash the ideas, imagination and creativity of its research employees. As already referred to in Chapter 7, however, top management fell short of exploiting the revolutionary ideas which emerged, i.e. the mouse, personal computer, laser printer, lap-top computer. Despite the changes they had made to increase quality and customer service, and the innovative ideas of its research employees, the company failed to innovate greatly in the market-place, leaving it vulnerable to fast moving global competition in the long term.

Common management misunderstandings 2

Although the company had begun to change its traditional hierarchical and 'arrogant' culture, the events indicate that the following perceptions had still not been overcome:

- Senior managers have knowledge and decision-making powers which are superior to that in other employees.
- Senior managers have knowledge and decision-making powers which are superior to that in customers.
- Success depends primarily on senior managers (and not front-line staff).

General lesson

> Western TQ philosophy, by concentrating on the broad rhetoric of culture change:
> *leadership, teamwork, vertical to horizontal structure, manager as teacher and coach, employee empowerment, customer care and satisfaction, etc.,*
> has failed adequately to address and promote core practical skills necessary to remove confusion and deliver the rhetoric down on the ground.

Further progress in Xerox

There is an awareness in management of many of the company's shortcomings in changing its culture: a prerequisite for on-going improvement. For example, a senior manager at Rank Xerox commented over 10 years after the inception of their quality programme:[3]

I recognised [about three years ago] that the challenge was to take quality improvement, TQM, from a level that I'd wrongly perceived as a task-orientated ideal, you know, how do I improve my task, to actually transform the *whole* company, the whole transformation of the way the company works, as opposed to what I would call a quality improvement team-type approach, suggestion schemes, all that stuff had been done. But what we were not really doing was addressing the *fundamental* enterprise and the culture of the whole enterprise … We've got a vertical thinking, and it was that realization that companies were not going to survive in a rapidly changing world unless they moved from a vertical to a horizontal orientation, that fascinated me intellectually.

The training manager referred to above acknowledged that although in some areas the company has been very successful in introducing greater employee involvement, for example in the form of self-managed work groups, extending involvement and self-team learning to all employees is still seen as a challenge. A senior manager at Xerox pointed out that the company is now integrating the work of its scientists directly into the company's business strategy for the first time. At Rank Xerox in the early 1990s there has been training in leadership and management style for senior managers. The Rank Xerox group personnel director acknowledged that the concept of a learning organization is a model which they are keen to adopt. A new coaching programme changing emphasis from traditional training to a mentoring model is being piloted by the board at Rank Xerox as an example to the rest of the workforce. Also, there is now a move to 'open things up' in Rank Xerox by having regular round-table discussions between senior managers, line managers and employees.

Learning culture implementation

The above example is representative of those Western companies that have had greatest success implementing a TQ approach. That is, even though, unlike the majority of companies, they have begun to dismantle the old bureaucratic and hierarchical culture, for the reasons given above they have fallen short of fully achieving the TQ philosophy and rhetoric. In particular, although in general there is talk about culture change and the need for:

- employee involvement and empowerment
- the transformation of the role of the manager to that of teacher and coach necessary to facilitate employee involvement
- the corresponding change from a hierarchical bureaucratic structure to a more horizontal, participative, cross-functional team structure

for improving quality and customer satisfaction, the development of the key 'interactive skills' necessary for achieving these goals has not been given full consideration and prominence in quality training programmes.

The outcome has been the tendency to continue to marginalize the importance of interpersonal skills in practice, and this inevitably will have undermined these companies' otherwise important moves to increase employee involvement, in turn working against their ability to deliver quality and innovation. It indicates that, at the time of writing, there is still some way to go before the leadership of such companies reaches the levels of humility, respect, ability to listen, and the other collaborative attitudes and skills, vital for the full harnessing of employee potential for maximizing efficiency, quality and innovation needed for long-term survival.

The lesson of past 'successful' TQ implementation

However strong the rhetoric and intention on culture change and empowerment, it will not easily be implemented even when there is commitment and active involvement of the main power broker. Generally, the examples show that even when conditions 1, 2 and 3 of the broad implementation framework shown at the beginning of this chapter are met, there is still the risk of the culture change message being watered down by the strength of ingrained traditional hierarchical attitudes and perceptions.

This necessitates the addition of a fourth condition to the implementation framework, namely:

4 The full integration of collaborative interpersonal skills development into the action programme from the outset, i.e. not as an add-on, an afterthought, but built into the whole learning/working process.

In other words, the whole action programme would need to incorporate the training–working team format (Aid 10,1; see Chapter 12). Otherwise, the key role of interpersonal skills and the culture change they enable is likely to be marginalized, and training dominated by task-orientated skills. Furthermore, condition 4 underpins the other 3 requirements indicated at the beginning of this chapter for implementing a learning culture.

Condition 4 is the pivotal component which fully ensures conditions 1, 2 and 3 of the implementation framework.

Satisfying all four conditions of the implementation framework, therefore, is the quickest and most effective route to maximizing efficiency, quality and innovation. It will save companies years of missed opportunities, wasted time and expense; and it is paramount for long-term survival against keen global competition.

Notes   1. Information in the following and in part of the subsequent Exercise
            from: interview with a training manager, Rank Xerox (UK), 1994;
            Total Quality: Transforming the Company Seminar, background
            reading, Rank Xerox (UK), March 1993. The interpretations are this
            author's.
         2. From: Kearney (1991) (see Reference); *Total Quality Management: a
            business process perspective*. A.T. Kearney, Inc., Chicago, 1992; *Creating
            the Environment for Total Quality Management*. A.T. Kearney, Inc.,
            Chicago, 1991.
         3. Quotation from: *In Business*, BBC Radio 4, 31 March 1993. Other
            information from comments by senior managers in: *In Business*, Radio
            4, 16 October 1994; 'Rank Insider', in *Personnel Today*, October 1994,
            pp.22-23.

Reference   Kearney A.T. (1991). *Total Quality: Time to Take Off the Rose-tinted
            Spectacles*, the results of a survey conducted by A.T. Kearney in
            association with *The TQM Magazine*. (A.T. Kearney Ltd, London)

12 Building a learning culture

This final chapter will consider how the collaborative team format indicated in Chapter 10:

- Can be used by top managers to build a non-judgemental culture, unleashing critical feedback, questioning and ideas, as a basis for continuous learning, creativity and innovation
- Highlights ineffective traditional downward and more recent upward and 360 degree 'add-on' appraisal techniques
- Enables cost-effective, integrated and continuous self-team appraisal
- Automatically and fully harnesses diversity of thought to create added-value for the customer

Initiating the action programme

Building trust quickly

The action programme recommended in Chapter 11 should begin with a training workshop (2 to 3 days in length) for the CEO with his or her team. The trainer should deploy the team format in line with the training framework indicated in Figure 10.1, and make clear:

- The team format's use as:
  - a vehicle for developing the core attitudes and skills of leadership, teamwork and learning;
  - a model for continued use within workplace meetings.
- The need for the top manager (CEO) to make structural changes to re-enforce the learning process (see later).

This training needs to be repeated for each team member and their teams, until all managers and supervisors have been involved. If the top manager is genuinely committed to change (see below), the 'training' will automatically continue in the workplace through the deployment of the team format in regular group meetings, which would build core team-learning skills development. However, the initial training will only be successful as a trigger to developing a learning culture if the following occurs.

Leading by example

The top manager will need to show a genuine commitment to deploying the team format from the outset, i.e. during his involvement in the training workshop, by being prepared to work at:

- Refraining from giving his or her own views before encouraging the expression of, and listening to, the views and ideas from the senior managers in the team.
- Encouraging team members to evaluate and develop their ideas.
- Allowing team members to question his or her beliefs, ideas, solutions.
- Encouraging team members to come up with their own solutions to problems.
- Welcoming and being willing to neutrally listen to and discuss views and ideas which oppose his or her own, and not take it as a personal affront.
- Encouraging team members to air their anxieties, concerns and mistakes, and tackle them constructively.
- Welcoming open honest feedback (matched against the aids in Chapter 10), on his or her performance of leading the team, such as:
  - I thought you spent too much time talking initially.
  - I felt you were not really listening when we suggested ideas which were different from your own.
  - You omitted to write up some suggestions and seemed not to be taking our suggestions seriously.
  - I thought you ended with your own conclusion/decision instead of seeking a group decision.
  - I thought what you said seemed a bit harsh and judgemental.
  - There was lack of eye contact and a facial expression which came over as disapproving.
  - Some of your questions, although they might seem open, I felt were closed, e.g. 'What could you do to actually address that?', and some came over as an attack because of an abrasive tone of voice, e.g. 'Why do you think that?!'

The top manager would also have to show that he or she is committed to continuing the approach in workplace meetings. Involvement of the top manager in this process is essential for:

- Developing the top manager's humility, tolerance and learning.
- Setting an example to senior team members of how they should behave with their teams, and so on down the line.
- Indicating that he or she is *serious* about culture change, necessary for developing a climate of trust, removing the fear of judgemental attack, disciplinary action or punitive reprisal (e.g. reduced bonuses, blocked promotion prospects, job loss), for suggesting opposing views and criticisms, admitting weaknesses, and making mistakes.

These outcomes of the above top management behaviour are the main building blocks for developing a learning culture.

> Behaviour will not change unless trust is built by the CEO—a major foundation of learning, added-value and profitability.

Unless the top manager sets this example, nobody will be convinced that he or she is serious about building a learning culture. A climate of fear will remain, with the consequence that the training of team members and their teams will be an expensive facade, and the action to implement and build a learning culture will fail.

Structural re-enforcement

To re-enforce the top manager's commitment to culture change and people's trust in it, he or she will need to back up the training by putting in place a structure along the lines indicated in Chapter 6, including:

- *Immediately seeing that teams are set up throughout the organization* involving every employee, and setting the example from the outset by having regular informal meetings with his or her team. (Teams should have interchanging members, depending on work projects being undertaken, and team leaders should be part of a broader team involving at least one senior manager, to ensure full communication and common goal setting.)
- *Clearly communicating the expectation that managers and supervisors will change their role* to coaching and developing team members, and *giving verbal recognition and practical support* to those that do.
- *Giving verbal recognition and practical support to employees* who enthusiastically take part in team meetings, questioning, coming up with ideas, evaluating and being involved in the decision-making process.
- *Removing individual financial reward and promotion systems* based on status, position, promotion politics, e.g. looking good in the eyes of the boss, ability to be autocratic, etc.

In addition, the top manager will need to:

- *Give priority to directing funds towards training, equipment, and R&D*, as a basis for providing general job security necessary for learning etc. (see Chapter 6).

Once a top manager takes the above actions relating to training and structure, a climate of trust will begin to develop. Under these conditions, and with the reassurance that the change will not mean managers losing their jobs, most managers will be able to develop from their role of cop to one of coach, teacher, mentor, and facilitator.

> Simultaneous structural changes are essential for cost-effective culture-change training and development.

There may be one or two people in management roles, however, who have deeply ingrained hierarchical attitudes and who therefore find it extremely difficult not to be distant and operate autocratically and dictatorially with subordinates. They should be offered further support and coaching, ideally from peer managers who are making the transition effectively. It should be made clear to them that if they are unable to start making changes, then it would be better from their own point of view and the organization's, that they do not work in a management role.

Building open feedback

Confrontational vs enquiry-based feedback

Open, honest feedback on individual performance and behaviour is needed for effective learning and innovation. Constructive positive feedback serves to motivate and reinforce effective and progressive ways of doing things. Constructive negative feedback serves to indicate where things have gone wrong, and provides a basis and motivation to consider how they could be improved. Neither occur to any extent in the traditional hierarchical organization due in the main to the following interrelated reasons:

- Managerial attitudes of arrogance, and the belief that his or her views are superior to those of subordinates.
- A belief that a weakness, having a problem, or making a mistake, are/ will be seen as a sign of innate inability in a person deserving reprisal.
- Distrust by managers (trainers, teachers) that acknowledging good performance in a subordinate is a threat to their own position: it will show them up as incompetent, and leave them open to blame and reprisal from above and below.
- Distrust by managers (trainers, teachers) that accepting negative feedback from subordinates will be seen as a sign of poor ability and incompetence, and lead to reprisal from above and below.

For these reasons managers (trainers, teachers):

- are unlikely to give positive feedback and praise subordinates
- do not encourage or easily countenance open negative feedback from subordinates, driving it underground into secret, unconstructive, negative criticism
- do not encourage subordinates to give open honest feedback about

their own weaknesses, problems and mistakes
- do not encourage subordinates to try things out and take risks
- are unlikely to be given open negative feedback from superiors, who tend to assess others secretly behind closed doors, when the manager (trainer, teacher) is not present to learn from it.

Without the moves by the top manager indicated in the previous section, the arrogance, distrust and fear characteristic of the traditional organization, both in industry and education, will not be allayed, however much rhetoric is directed at managers or employees, and however many workshops they attend. The prevailing traditional culture will block the process of open honest feedback, both in the area of leadership-team skills and general work issues. Neither manager nor subordinates will welcome it down on the ground.

Personalized reactions It is the 'macho' character of the traditional culture, i.e. arrogance combined with judgemental intolerance, which leads weaknesses and mistakes to be perceived as a sign of a person's innate inability deserving punitive reprisal. Negative feedback, therefore, is highly personalized and sensitized in such a culture. The traumatic nature of negative feedback in the traditional organization is reflected by the way the various emotions people go through when receiving it have been compared with the effects of bereavement (Figure 12.1).

Shock/denial	This can't be true. You've made a mistake. I don't want to hear it.	Traditional organization
Anger	What right have you got? Who told you that? I'm going to get them.	
Acceptance	May be there is room for improvement.	
Renewed action/ help	I will do that next time. Can you help? What do you suggest?	Learning organization

Figure 12.1 *Traumatic and constructive responses to negative feedback*

It is evident from the second 'anger' stage why subordinates dare not be open and honest. This portrayal of the effects of negative feedback omits the emotion of fear of reprisal when weaknesses are exposed. The emotion of fear, in fact, is likely to increase the first two emotions as defensive mechanisms.

The fact is in the traditional culture people (and in particular, managers) rarely get beyond the anger/fear stage, and a sense of resentment towards the person/s giving the feedback. Even if they come to accept the feedback, and their awareness of how they come over to subordinates is increased, it is rare for them to get to the next stage and act on it effectively merely on the basis of the particular feedback they receive (see appraisal section). Change is likely to be limited and peripheral to the underlying autocratic management process, e.g. listening a bit more, being a little less abrasive, a little more approachable. In the unlikely event that a manager does try to make fundamental changes (perhaps due to the fact that he or she had previously operated collaboratively in another organization), and moves to empower and involve subordinates equally in decision-making processes, the overriding effect of the general organizational culture will mean that he or she will meet resistance from below in the form of distrust, and from above (and possibly below) in the form of judgemental attack, such as incompetence, unable to do the job, etc.

Collaborative responses   In contrast, where a non-judgemental collaborative culture holds, and negative feedback, weaknesses and mistakes are, from the top, no longer associated with intrinsic inability and the allocation of blame and punishment, the first two stages of the traditional reaction path drop out (Figure 12.1). Fear is removed and therefore people are not as defensive. Reinforcing this, arrogance is replaced by humility and self-appraisal from the top. As a result both managers and subordinates welcome and are able to give, open negative feedback, and see it purely as a basis to solve problems and help improve the individual's (and the group's) future understanding, learning and future performance. In this kind of culture people feel they are part of a supportive learning community (see also Chapter 8)

> Different ideas should be expressed and critically discussed to give the best solution. It's not adversarial, that I want to hurt, destroy or overrun you.
>
> *Honda employee*

Example: negative feedback in the traditional culture   A student complained to me about negative feedback in the final written report she received at the end of a practical course on presentation/teaching skills:

I asked whether I was doing alright, and was told 'yes'.

Why didn't (the trainer) say something to me?

If I had been told earlier I could have done something about it.

The student's frustration and annoyance clearly indicated that she saw the negative feedback constructively, and that withholding it had meant that a learning opportunity had been missed. In contrast, her assessor, by avoiding giving face to face feedback (possibly to spare the student's feelings), indicated that he or she saw it as a judgement on the student's lack of ability which was innate and therefore unchangeable.

Another student complained:

The only feedback I get is negative.

I felt there was no point in trying.

This suggested that the feedback had been given unconstructively, again indicating that the trainer had viewed it as a fixed judgement against the student's ability: a perception which was in the process of being transferred to the student, demotivating and blocking learning and improvement.

A third student, in the final year of a 3-year course that I had not previously been involved in, thanked me for giving him direct negative feedback which he had found useful. Over the previous years, it seems, he had received no constructive face to face feedback, despite being given poor reports about his performance and 'manner'. Once again, a closed decision seemed to have been made about the student's ability.

Depersonalizing feedback

The use of the aids (Chapter 10) to give feedback within the above described action programme, helps the process of depersonalizing it by:

- The receiver of the feedback knowing that it is being judged against a set of objective criteria/procedures.
- Enabling the giver to use less personal, more fact-based language.

For example, the seemingly highly personal and provocative statement:

'I do not find you helpful.'

becomes:

'I did not find ⎰ the suggestions you made / the way you seemed not to listen to my concerns/suggestions / the way you did not seek my views / etc. ⎱ helpful.'

helping feedback become less of a judgement against the person and more an appraisal of a situation.

Encourage self-appraisal

When the response is from manager to subordinate, mentor to mentee, in order to further ensure that confrontation is avoided and to enhance the coach/teacher role, the manager should first attempt to encourage self-appraisal and elicit an evaluation from the subordinate through the use of open questions (see also next section), rather than go straight in to giving direct negative feedback. For example, the process could begin by asking:

How would you describe what happened?

How do you think you did? (matched against standard procedures, agreed goals)

Other open questions of the kind indicated in Aid 10.3 can be used to explore the situation. Direct negative feedback can effectively be given after the self-appraisal process, if the latter does not highlight main shortcomings. Often, however, it does, rendering direct negative feedback unnecessary. Even if direct negative feedback is used, it should be followed by open questions to encourage self-appraisal of future action, such as:

What would you do differently in future?

How do you think you can make improvements?

These questions will be unnecessary if self-appraisal of future action is prompted either by the initial open questions, or the direct negative feedback. It is important to re-enforce or temper negative and positive self-appraisal; incorporate positive with negative feedback; and re-enforce sound ideas and suggestions for future action.

Feedback procedure checklist

1 **Ask open questions to evoke self-appraisal**
   e.g. 'How do you think it went?'

   Follow by further exploratory questions
   e.g. Why do you think that happened?'

   Re-enforce or temper positive and negative self-appraisal
   e.g. 'Yes, I thought that was very effective.'
      'Yes, I agree that aspect could be improved.'
      'I think you are being a bit hard on yourself, that wasn't too bad.'

2 **Give direct negative feedback** (if 1 does not elicit main shortcomings)
   e.g. 'I felt you could have improved on ...'

   Include feedback to highlight and re-enforce any positive aspects

3 **Ask open questions to evoke self-appraisal of future action**
   (unless 1 or 2 leads to it).
   e.g. 'How would you do it differently next time?'

   Re-enforce sound ideas and suggestions
   e.g. 'Yes, I think that would be better.'
      'Yes, go ahead.'

Self-appraisal of future action, allowing trainee/student/employee to be involved in deciding future action and goals, is a powerful vehicle for fostering commitment to improved performance. Figure 12.2 contrasts

(a) *Traditional confrontational feedback*
• judgemental, intolerant, secretive • received (and often given) as a personal attack against an individual's innate ability • seen as a fixed, static, unchangeable assessment, leaving no room for improvement • generally confrontational, adversarial, used as a basis to allocate blame and punishment • unwelcomed and inhibited, blocking opportunities to learn, solve problems, and improve performance
(b) *Collaborative enquiry-based feedback*
• non-judgemental, tolerant, open • not personalized, i.e. not given or received as a judgement on innate ability • considered as a transitional evaluation of performance to help understanding and improvement • enquiry-based and supportive, facilitating employee involvement, creativity and risk taking • welcomed as a basis for learning, solving problems and innovating

Figure 12.2 *Negative feedback in traditional and learning organizations*

key features relating to negative feedback in a traditional and learning organization.

Building imagination, intellect and innovation

The freedom and time (see below) to reflect, critically question and come up with ideas and suggestions which challenge the *status quo*, are essential for fuelling the imagination, and for bringing about effective learning, creativity and innovation. As in the case of open feedback, however, these are blocked in the traditional hierarchical organization, and for the same reasons.

Keep asking questions?

External trainers, educationalists and consultants on learning, who exhort employees, trainees and students to 'keep asking questions' in order fully to understand and learn effectively, are being naive and unrealistic. They fail to realize just how difficult this is for most people to do in the majority of working and training/education organizations. Because of factors considered in the previous section, such as:

• management attitudes of arrogance; the belief that managers' ideas are superior to those of subordinates; the fear of judgemental punitive reprisal if 'shown up' by subordinates; the concern with disciplinary action and punishment if weaknesses are exposed, there is a high level of personalization, and the chances are that if a subordinate asks a question, his or her superior will see it as one, or a combination, of the following:

- A sign of impertinence/lack of deference.
- An attack against the superior's competence and authority.
- A sign of unhelpfulness and rocking the boat.
- A sign of inability and lack of intelligence in the subordinate (this can be the case both when the question arises out of lack of understanding, *and* when it poses a valid point which the manager/trainer had previously not thought of and/or which challenges orthodoxy).

The first three perceptions can be the case even when the question is not directly related to the superior's actions and performance. Exactly the same applies in the training-educational setting as the work setting. People who are considered as model employees, trainees and students, are likely to be those who do not ask 'awkward' or 'stupid' questions. The reaction I received in one job interview in the past amusingly revealed this tendency. There was a decided dampening of the interviewers' enthusiasm when I commented, relating to the way I go about working, 'I ask a lot of questions'.

Keep suggesting ideas?

Similarly, and for the same reasons given above, if a subordinate makes a suggestion, and comes up with an idea which the manager/trainer had previously not thought of, or which is new and opposes the accepted wisdom, it will often be seen as a sign of impertinence; an attack on the superior's competence and authority; unhelpful and awkward; or a sign of inability and poor intelligence (this latter can be the reaction not just when the idea is invalid, but also when it is valid and challenging). Again, model employees and students and are likely to be considered to be those who do not make 'threatening', 'stupid' or 'silly' suggestions.

Unleashing questioning and ideas

This does not occur in the traditional organization, therefore. Employees and trainees are not encouraged to ask questions or make suggestions, and because of the threat of punishment, generally fear doing so. Instead, they play safe and avoid the risk of considering new and improved ways of doing things (see also Chapter 6). The spirit of enquiry, therefore, together with the learning and innovation it enables, is stunted. In contrast, building collaborative attitudes/skills such as trust, humility and tolerance through the route discussed in this chapter:

- breaks down the anti-learning blocks of arrogance, distrust and fear of reprisal
- removes the feeling that people are above you or below you, and builds mutual respect and equality
- builds confidence, unleashing questioning and suggesting of ideas.

> A culture of trust, humility and tolerance ensures that questions and ideas are never irrationally discouraged, ridiculed or reprimanded.

Encourage imagination

With questions such as the following, asked in an open way, i.e. *genuinely seeking and respecting* what the employees/trainees might come up with so that they know they will be *listened to*, managers/trainers will encourage imagination, ideas and suggestions.

Manager/trainer questions

What do you think?
Why should that be?
How can this be improved?
Why should it be done this way rather than some other way?

(See also top and bottom of Aid 10.3.)

In addition to attentive, respectful listening, the manager/trainer should visually record all responses. This is an important vehicle which:

- re-enforces the employees'/trainees' belief that their views are being taken seriously, boosting self-confidence and encouraging imagination
- helps remove inhibitions and free the imagination by giving all ideas a fair hearing, even though some might turn out to be invalid, or initially seem silly and 'way-out'
- facilitates subsequent evaluation of ideas (see below), avoiding the confusion which arises by relying on people's memories of what has been suggested.

Encourage enquiry

The use of such open questions will also show employees/trainees that it is acceptable to ask questions. It will, therefore, encourage and prompt questioning such as the following by employees/trainees to increase understanding on a number of levels, and these should be welcomed by the manager/trainer.

Employee/trainee questions of:

● *Clarification*	I don't understand, can you explain that again?
	Did you say ... or ...?
● *Exploration*	Why should that be the case?
	Why should that happen rather than ...?
	Why do you do it this way rather than that?
● *Broad exploration*	What are we doing?
	How are we doing it?
	Why are we doing it?

These questioning processes overlap and occur continuously within the team format (Aid 10.1); and employees/trainees will ask the exploration questions of themselves and the manager/trainer. The questioning by employees/trainees will, of course, be a basis for further ideas, hypothesizing ('what if ...?'), suggesting, and innovating. Employees/ trainees should be encouraged to write down their ideas and views which occur outside group meetings to enhance knowledge and understanding, and to fix new ideas for the next group meeting (see also Chapter 8).

Building intellect   To ensure that the ideas suggested are sound, and to focus down to those most likely to lead to effective solutions and innovations, the manager/trainer needs to 'feed' rationality into the enquiry process, developing the employees'/trainees' reasoning skills as a basis for rigorous evaluation of the ideas. This will include trying to get employees/trainees to:

- become aware of their assumptions
- fully consider/present the reasons to justify their views
- consider and weigh up alternatives
- explore the implications of what they suggest

as a basis for building on one another's ideas. This can be done through the use of open questions exemplified in Aid 10.3.

The process of continuous enquiry initiated through genuine deployment of the team format as described above, is summarized in Figure 12.3. Through on-going questioning by all participants, therefore, understanding will be increased, solutions to problems will be reached, and innovative ideas will be created.

> Only if the traditional judgemental culture changes, will people *be able to* 'stick their necks out'—give open honest feedback, critically question, seek and listen to negative feedback (internally and externally), come up with ideas, admit problems, experiment, make mistakes, fail, etc.—and will learning, innovation, and value for the customer be maximized.

The time factor   A common response in traditional hierarchical organizations is that deploying the team format in the working and training environments— involving, fully informing, consulting, giving feedback, etc.—would take up too much extra time which organizations can ill afford. This view arises because people are unable to think outside the traditional paradigm; often it is those people in positions of power who are more strongly imbued with the hierarchical attitudes and 'skills' (Figure 5.2).

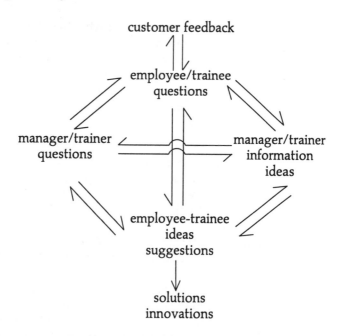

Figure 12.3 *Reinforcing circles of questions and ideas*

True, it would 'slow everything down' and 'waste time' if it were just a case of more people spending time talking in groups, with little else changing. But, as this book considers, to be effective the approach requires far-reaching cultural and structural changes. Through these changes, time spent on employee/trainee involvement is more than compensated for by time savings brought about by increased efficiency as a result of increase in employee/trainee motivation and commitment: not to mention the increase in quality and innovation this, and only this, approach can achieve.

Traditional versus enquiry-based appraisal

Effective enquiry-based appraisal is only possible in a collaborative culture. Appraisal systems within the traditional hierarchical organization are at best limited and at worst ineffective and counterproductive.

Traditional downward appraisal

The traditional one-way appraisal technique where managers appraise employees, usually on a half-, one-, or two-yearly basis, has had little to do with an objective appraisal of performance. Generally it has been used judgementally as a means of enforcing management control and discipline. It has evoked in employees responses of defensiveness, secretiveness, dejection and fear of reprisal. Also, because of the personal nature of the appraisal which largely neglects objective factors that affect performance, together with the fact that managers are often distant from their subordinates and therefore have an inaccurate and biased perception of what they have done, appraisal reports tend to be inaccurate and unfair. Negative reports therefore are met with cynicism. As a result traditional downward appraisal has been counterproductive, undermining rather than facilitating individual and organizational improvement; and rewards based on this approach, such as performance-related pay are divisive, and can lead to discord and conflict.

The move by some organizations to include feedback from the employee during the appraisal interview is largely cosmetic and manipulative. Without a move to change the overall culture, employees will remain cynical and fearful, and will hold back from open, honest feedback.

Upward appraisal   The technique of appraisal of managers by their subordinates reverses the traditional approach. In Britain in the early 1990s it was heralded by some as a revolutionary new technique empowering employees, although it had been around for decades in America where it originated. As in the case of downward appraisal, this technique is a one-way process, and is typically applied as an add-on to the traditional hierarchical culture at periodic intervals with often long gaps in between. Employees are asked to 'assess' or 'mark' their manager's performance by anonymously completing a questionnaire. These mainly concentrate on skills which correspond to some of those at the functional level indicated in Figure 4.1, but occasionally there are questions directly referring to the lower level interpersonal skills and attitudes. For example:

Does your manager:

  - Delegate work effectively?
  - Clarify difficult problems?
  - Inform and keep you up to date with external issues?
  - Encourage individuals to find solutions?
  - Support, guide and train?
  - Listen to your concerns and ideas?
  - Enable you to say what you think?
  - Act fairly and honestly?
  - Act on commitments made?

Companies vary in what they do with the results of the survey. One company might expect managers to discuss the feedback with their teams. This is often with a member of the personnel department leading the discussion. Another company might not expect managers to discuss the feedback; might keep the analysis of the feedback confidential to the surveyed manager, his or her manager, and the training manager; and might put no pressure on managers to act on it.

Shortcomings of upward appraisal techniques

Major shortcomings include:

1 The use of an anonymous form in which employees are asked to 'assess' or 'mark' their manager, will tend to:
   (a) facilitate unconstructive personal judgemental attack, and unfair over-reaction;
   (b) reinforce secrecy and the fact that the culture is one where honest feedback cannot be open;
   (c) reinforce the barrier between managers and subordinates;
   (d) reinforce fear, apprehensiveness and defensiveness in the manager.

2 The use of the personnel department as a 'mediator' between managers and their teams—receiving, analyzing and controlling the feedback to the manager—reinforces the negative aspects under 1 above.

3 The use of someone from the personnel department to lead any feedback meeting with subordinates, and the requirement that the manager merely listens, reinforces the divide between the manager and the subordinates and increases the confrontational nature of the meeting.

4 The inevitability that any feedback meeting will be tense and strained on both sides, and the amount of open honest negative feedback within the meeting will be limited.

5 The use of the technique as an add-on with gaps in between, reinforces the perception that honest feedback is not expected to occur continuously in the workplace.

6 The limited domain of the process, i.e. appraisal of the manager's team-leadership skills, excludes appraisal of team members' performance and other work issues (some of which might need to be fed back higher up the line).

7 The possibility of its use as a judgemental tool to police the behaviour of managers as a basis for financial reward or punishment, or to reduce numbers of managers, thereby increasing managers' fears, and their likelihood of suppressing and rejecting negative feedback in order to present a favourable image.

The above negative aspects construe to make the process far from empowering for the employee, and the feedback information of little value to the manager. It might increase awareness in some managers of some of their own weaknesses, but as considered in the previous section, they will not necessarily act on this, and if they do the change will be marginal.

A list indicating what a manager might be doing wrong at the functional and core interpersonal levels, such as that provided by upward feedback questionnaires, is no guide to action, even if the manager accepts and attempts to act on the feedback. It does not indicate *how in practice* they can go about changing. What is required is an analysis of the core skills and underlying attitudes needed for effective change (Chapter 4), a structured practical procedure for developing these core skills (Chapter 10), and action by the top manager (indicated above) to encourage and enable the deployment of these procedures throughout the organization.

Not cost effective   Some companies have spent millions of pounds implementing programmes of upward feedback alongside training workshops for groups of their managers, using the feedback to highlight training needs. However, as considered above and in Chapter 10 relating to the training of groups of middle managers, these will have a limited effect on changing the role of the manager from cop to coach. At best they are not a cost-effective use of funds, and at worst they are highly wasteful.

The 360 degree appraisal   This technique uses the opinions of superiors, peers and subordinates to appraise managers. The aim is to get a fuller picture of a manager's strengths and weaknesses. As in the case of upward appraisal, it is questionnaire based and essentially one-way: from others to the manager. It has all the fundamental shortcomings indicated above for upward appraisal.

> Despite high promise and expense, upward and 360 degree appraisal techniques are typically used as 'add-ons' which, in themselves, can have little effect on management and organizational performance.

In short, such appraisal techniques will be no more than an expensive tinkering on the margins unless there is culture change from the top of an organization as described at the beginning of this chapter.

Self-team appraisal   The initial training workshop referred to at the beginning of this chapter, starting with the top manager's (CEO) use of the collaborative team format (Aid 10.1) with his or her team, will set rolling the following appraisal processes:

1 Self-team appraisal of work issues—using the Aids (Chapter 10).
2 Team feedback of the team leader's leadership skills/attitudes—matched against the Aids (Chapter 10).
3 Self-team appraisal by each team member of their own and other's team skills/attitudes—matched against the Aids (Chapter 10).

It is the trust created by the example of the top manager's actions, referred to above, and the open, honest feedback it enables in the workplace, which ensures that such appraisal processes are effective. Through these processes the manager's role changes to coach, teacher, mentor. Working, 'training' and learning is two-way (Chapters 8 and

10), and traditional judgmental assessment systems are replaced by employee/trainee involvement in enquiry-based dialogue and collaborative evaluation as a basis for learning, future improvement and innovation.

Continuous, integrated appraisal

Time should be set aside during team meetings for 2 and 3, particularly at management levels at the beginning of the building process. This 'introspective' appraisal of leadership-team skills is, of course, the basis for effective appraisal and learning relating to other work issues (1). The advantage of the above prescribed approach is that it effectively integrates these appraisal processes with each other and within workplace activities.

> By developing a collaborative culture, self-team appraisal and the learning it enables becomes an integral and continuous part of workplace activities; and periodic, expensive, and ineffective add-on appraisal techniques are rendered redundant.

Summary of appraisal rationales

Downward appraisal: mainly to provide an assessment on which to base individual reward or punishment, and through which to enforce management control and discipline.

Upward and 360 degree appraisal: to provide managers with information to help them improve their management performance, and empower employees.

In reality, empowerment is limited to anonymous feedback/attack, and judgemental assessment remains an important element of these appraisal techniques, either as an underlying rationale or as a threat. This is indicated by their overt use in some organizations to influence pay, promotion and job security; and their use in other organizations alongside a traditional downward appraisal system.

Self-team appraisal: purely to provide a basis for collaboratively improving individual and group performance and innovation.

Comparison between appraisal approaches in the different cultures—hierarchical and collaborative—is summarized in Figure 12.4.

Traditional hierarchical culture

Appraisal technique	Characteristic	Feedback	Outcome
Downward	• one-way • add-on • periodic • formal	• mainly not sought • strained (if open) • threatening (Fig. 12.2a)	• ineffective • counter-productive • undermines future performance • highly wasteful
Upward 360 degree	• one-way • add-on • periodic • formal	• anonymous • strained (if open) • threatening (Fig. 12.2.a)	*at best* • limited effect on performance • not cost-effective *at worst* • counter-productive • highly wasteful

Collaborative learning culture

Appraisal technique	Characteristic	Feedback	Outcome
Self-team	• two-way • integrated • continuous • informal	• open • relaxed • enquiry-based (Fig. 12.2b)	• effective for learning and innovation • cost-effective

Figure 12.4 *Appraisal techniques in different cultures*

Democratic harnessing of diversity

Traditional suppression of diversity

Underlying attitudes and 'skills' of the traditional hierarchical culture: disrespect, distrust, arrogance, non-listening, secrecy, judgemental intolerance, irrationality, etc., have been previously identified to be at the root of the exclusion of the majority of employees from decision-making processes. They have formed:

• a barrier between manager and employee
• reduced morale and commitment in those who suffer from exclusion

- self-interest and rivalry between employee and employee
- greatest exclusion and marginalization of those who conform least to the dominant white, male, middle class model.

Excluded people, as has been considered, do not perform as well as they could do, do not contribute as much as they could do, do not learn effectively and do not give their best to the organization. Generally, this has always been the case for the majority of employees, traditionally white working class males. The widespread belief by managers that subordinates have a lower ability has already been referred to. This is backed up by further beliefs such as:

- People with lower educational achievements have lower ability.
- People who are illiterate or semi-literate have lower ability.
- People who have dyslexia have lower ability.

These beliefs are mistaken. They are based on prejudicial ignorance and arrogance. The director general of the CBI, for example, has expressed concern that dyslexics are underperforming in the workplace as a result of barriers which could be removed by management, and that this represents a great loss in potential and creativity for businesses. Exactly the same point, unfortunately, can be said for most working people. Prejudice has been rife in the traditional organizational culture.

Yet, it is only as demographic changes and globalization leads to greater diversity in the nature of the workforce, particularly in terms of gender and race, that there is growing awareness and concern over employee exclusion and marginalization, and the extent to which it represents a huge wasted potential to organizations.

The growth in courses and programmes relating to 'valuing diversity', in fact, is an indictment of the long-standing exclusiveness within the traditional organization. However, as pointed out previously, education and training programmes cannot be effective in themselves, and they will be undermined in the workplace unless prevailing hierarchical cultures and structures are changed.

> Unless organizations are able to overcome the barriers and prejudices which have traditionally excluded the majority of white working class male employees, there is little chance of them effectively harnessing the potential benefits of diversity in gender, race, physical ability and age.

Breaking down barriers and prejudices

The prejudice traditionally displayed by employees against minority groups is essentially an extension of the hierarchical relationship between managers and employees. Much of this book has considered how changing to a collaborative culture overcomes barriers and prejudices between managers and employees, to fully involve and empower the latter to work efficiently and effectively. At the root of these changes are core attitudes and skills which include: respect, trust, humility, listening, openness, non-judgemental tolerance, rationality, etc. It is the building of these through the deployment of the team format, as described above, that creates a non-judgemental climate of reflection and enquiry, and this automatically breaks down destructive intolerance and prejudices against minority groups. A major aspect of this is the challenging of assumptions.

Challenging underlying
assumptions

This involves:

- Open questions from team leader, manager, or trainer to elicit the airing of views, beliefs and prejudices (Aid 10.3).
- Open questions from team leader to encourage people to consider and tolerate alternative beliefs and views.
- Peer feedback and questioning, challenging prejudices expressed.
- Open questions from team leader to ensure: consideration of underlying assumptions, reasons and evidence; consistency and relevance; consideration of the implications of views and beliefs (Aid 10.3). (Some of these aspects will come through peer feedback.)

Peer feedback and questioning is very powerful for:

- promoting self-reflection, awareness, and self-questioning
- promoting fair and rational consideration of different perspectives
- developing understanding and tolerance.

In so doing, it breaks down barriers, overcomes prejudices and stereotyping, and creates a supportive, harmonious and listening community which values all contributions.

Within the building process, the team leader him or herself will also have preconceived ideas and prejudices. The process of learning to deploy the team format, of hanging back, being silent, listening to what someone has to say, and encouraging evaluation of a situation before rushing in and imposing his or her own beliefs, teaches the team leader to question and evaluate their own assumptions, prejudices, and preconceived solutions to problems.

This democratic process ensures that the full potential of diversity of thought in all employees is tapped and mobilized, regardless of class, race, gender, physical ability, age, etc. Harnessing different perspectives from a divergence of class, race, gender, age, physical ability, etc., ensures an effective consideration of end-customer needs and requirements.

The key features relating to the response to diversity in the two different cultures: traditional and learning, are summarized in Figure 12.5.

Traditional culture

- intolerant, divisive, individualistic
- blocks diversity of feedback, questions and ideas, undermining learning and innovation
- channels people's energies into destructive prejudice, subversion, rivalry, and personal gain
- mainly wastes the potential of employees to take feedback from, and add-value for, the customer.

Learning culture

- supportive, harmonious, collaborative
- values diversity of feedback, questioning and suggesting as the key to continuous learning and innovation
- focuses people's energies on working together to solve problems and make improvements
- taps and mobilizes the potential of all employees to work closely with, and produce added-value in products, processes, and service for the benefit of, the customer.

Figure 12.5 *Opposing cultural responses to diversity*

Summary: training do's and don'ts

The following lists the key things that can be done to avoid wasteful training and promote continuous learning and cost-effective training.

Don't

- Have a separate training, HR, or quality department
- Send employees away to 'off-the-peg' external courses
- Send middle managers/trainers on external or in-house courses/ workshops relating to leadership, teamwork, empowerment, quality, or customer care
- Have add-on quality systems
- Bring in external consultants to train middle managers
- Use artificial training approaches - fictional examples and team games, contrived exercises and puzzles, outdoor activities
- Use downward or upward appraisal and related pay schemes
- Disproportionately direct funds to top salaries, share dividends, perks, administration, office equipment, etc., at the expense of training and development
- Have inflexible job descriptions, distinctions and demarcations
- Use authoritarian, one-way, lecture-based training

Do

- Devolve decisions for learning and training
- Promote as far as possible work-based training by line managers
- Work in partnership with external providers to create flexible, tailor-made, work-related, training
- Develop integrated work-based leadership-team training for all managers/trainers *with their teams* from the top as part of learning culture development
- Only bring in a consultant if needed to help facilitate the above work-based leadership-team development
- Create a supportive internal network of trainers, backed up as far as

is possible by easy access to learning resources/a flexible learning centre
- Create a fair pay system and, as far as possible, job security
- Always promote and use collaborative, two-way, enquiry-based training and development

Index

Further titles in the McGraw-Hill Training Series

All books are published by:

McGraw-Hill Book Company Europe
Shoppenhangers Road, Maidenhead, Berkshire SL6 2QL, England
Tel: (01628) 23432   Fax: (01628) 770224